Bulletin of the
Philosophical Society
of Washington
Vol. IV

Also from Westphalia Press

westphaliapress.org

Bulletin of the Philosophical Society of Washington

Vol. IV

From The Philosophical Society of Washington Minutes

1880-1881

WESTPHALIA PRESS

An imprint of Policy Studies Organization

Bulletin of the Philosophical Society of Washington, Vol. IV
All Rights Reserved © 2014 by Policy Studies Organization

Westphalia Press
An imprint of Policy Studies Organization
1527 New Hampshire Ave., NW
Washington, D.C. 20036
info@ipsonet.org

ISBN-13: 978-1-63391-069-0
ISBN-10: 1633910695
Cover design by Taillefer Long at Illuminated Stories:
www.illuminatedstories.com

Daniel Gutierrez-Sandoval, Executive Director
PSO and Westphalia Press

Devin Proctor, Director of Media and Publications
PSO and Westphalia Press

Updated material and comments on this edition
can be found at the Westphalia Press website:
www.westphaliapress.org

BULLETIN

OF THE

PHILOSOPHICAL SOCIETY

OF

WASHINGTON.

VOL. IV.

Containing the Minutes of the Society from the 185th Meeting,
October 9, 1880, to the 202d Meeting, June 11, 1881.

PUBLISHED BY THE CO-OPERATION OF THE SMITHSONIAN INSTITUTION.

WASHINGTON
1881.

CONTENTS.

CONSTITUTION

OF

THE PHILOSOPHICAL SOCIETY OF WASHINGTON.

ARLICLE I. The name of this Society shall be THE PHILOSOPHICAL SOCIETY OF WASHINGTON.

ARTICLE II. The officers of the Society shall be a President, four Vice-Presidents, a Treasurer, and two Secretaries.

ARTICLE III. There shall be a General Committee, consisting of the officers of the Society and nine other members.

ARTICLE IV. The officers of the Society and the other members of the General Committee shall be elected annually by ballot; they shall hold office until their successors are elected, and shall have power to fill vacancies.

ARTICLE V. It shall be the duty of the General Committee to make rules for the government of the Society, and to transact all its business.

ARTICLE VI. This constitution shall not be amended except by a three-fourths vote of those present at an annual meeting for the election of officers, and after notice of the proposed change shall have been given in writing at a stated meeting of the Society at least four weeks previously.

STANDING RULES

FOR THE GOVERNMENT OF THE

PHILOSOPHICAL SOCIETY OF WASHINGTON.

JANUARY, 1881.

---

1. The Stated Meetings of the Society shall be held at 8 o'clock P. M. on every alternate Saturday; the place of meeting to be designated by the General Committee.

2. Notice of the time and place of meeting shall be sent to each member by one of the Secretaries.

When necessary, Special Meetings may be called by the President.

3. The Annual Meeting for the election of officers shall be the last stated meeting in the month of December.

The order of proceedings (which shall be announced by the Chair) shall be as follows:

First, the reading of the minutes of the last Annual Meeting.

Second, the presentation of the annual reports of the Secretaries, including the announcement of the names of members elected since the last annual meeting.

Third, the presentation of the annual report of the Treasurer.

Fourth, the announcement of the names of members who having complied with Section 12 of the Standing Rules, are entitled to vote on the election of officers.

Fifth, the election of President.

Sixth, the election of four Vice-Presidents.

Seventh, the election of Treasurer.

Eighth, the election of two Secretaries.

Ninth, the election of nine members of the General Committee.

Tenth, the consideration of Amendments to the Constitution of the Society, if any such shall have been proposed in accordance with Article VI of the Constitution.

Eleventh, the reading of the rough minutes of the meeting.

4. Elections of officers are to be held as follows:

In each case nominations shall be made by means of an informal ballot, the result of which shall be announced by the Secretary; after which the first formal ballot shall be taken.

In the ballot for Vice-Presidents, Secretaries, and Members of the General Committee, each voter shall write on one ballot as many names as there are officers to be elected, viz., four on the first ballot for Vice-Presidents, two on the first for Secretaries, and nine on the first for Members of the General Committee; and on each subsequent ballot as many names as there are persons yet to be elected; and those persons who receive a majority of the votes cast shall be declared elected.

If in any case the informal ballot result in giving a majority for any one, it may be declared formal by a majority vote.

5. The Stated Meetings, with the exception of the annual meeting, shall be devoted to the consideration and discussion of scientific subjects.

The Stated Meeting next preceding the Annual Meeting shall be set apart for the delivery of the President's Annual Address.

6. Sections representing special branches of science may be formed by the General Committee upon the written recommendation of twenty members of the Society.

7. Persons interested in science, who are not residents of the District of Columbia, may be present at any meeting of the Society, except the annual meeting, upon invitation of a member.

8. Similar invitations to residents of the District of Columbia, not members of the Society, must be submitted through one of the Secretaries to the General Committee for approval.

9. Invitations to attend during three months the meetings of the Society and participate in the discussion of papers, may, by a vote of nine members of the General Committee, be issued to persons nominated by two members.

10. Communications intended for publication under the auspices of the Society shall be submitted in writing to the General Committee for approval.

11. New members may be proposed in writing by three members of the Society for election by the General Committee: but no person shall be admitted to the privileges of membership unless he signifies his acceptance thereof in writing within two months after notification of his election.

12. Each member shall pay annually to the Treasurer the sum of five dollars, and no member whose dues are unpaid shall vote at the annual meeting for the election of officers, or be entitled to a copy of the Bulletin.

In the absence of the Treasurer, the Secretary is authorized to receive the dues of members.

The names of those two years in arrears shall be dropped from the list of members.

Notice of resignation of membership shall be given in writing to the General Committee through the President or one of the Secretaries.

13. The fiscal year shall terminate with the Annual Meeting.

14. Members who are absent from the District of Columbia for more than twelve months may be excused from payment of the annual assessments, in which case their names shall be dropped from the list of members. They can, however, resume their membership by giving notice to the President of their wish to do so.

15. Any member not in arrears may, by the payment of one hundred dollars at any one time, become a life member, and be relieved from all further annual dues and other assessments.

All moneys received in payment of life membership shall be invested as portions of a permanent fund, which shall be directed solely to the furtherance of such special scientific work as may be ordered by the General Committee.

STANDING RULES

OF THE

GENERAL COMMITTEE OF THE PHILOSOPHICAL SOCIETY OF WASHINGTON.

JANUARY, 1881.

---

1. The President, Vice-Presidents, and Secretaries of the Society shall hold like offices in the General Committee.

2. The President shall have power to call special meetings of the Committee, and to appoint Sub-Committees.

3. The Sub-Committees shall prepare business for the General Committee, and perform such other duties as may be entrusted to them.

4. There shall be two Standing Sub-Committees; one on Communications for the Stated Meetings of the Society, and another on Publications.

5. The General Committee shall meet at half-past seven o'clock on the evening of each Stated Meeting, and by adjournment at other times.

6. For all purposes except for the amendment of the Standing Rules of the Committee or of the Society, and the election of members, six members of the Committee shall constitute a quorum.

7. The names of proposed new members recommended in conformity with Section 11 of the Standing Rules of the Society, may be presented at any meeting of the General Committee, but shall lie over for at least four weeks before final action, and the concur-

rence of twelve members of the Committee shall be necessary to election.

The Secretary of the General Committee shall keep a chronological register of the elections and acceptances of members.

8. These Standing Rules, and those for the government of the Society, shall be modified only with the consent of a majority of the members of the General Committee.

RULES

PUBLICATION OF THE BULLETIN

OF THE

PHILOSOPHICAL SOCIETY OF WASHINGTON.

JANUARY, 1881.

---

1. The President's annual address shall be published in full.

2. The annual reports of the Secretaries and of the Treasurer shall be published in full.

3. When directed by the General Committee, any communication may be published in full.

4. Abstracts of papers and remarks on the same will be published, when presented to the Secretary by the author in writing within two weeks of the evening of their delivery, and approved by the Committee on Publications. Brief abstracts prepared by one of the Secretaries and approved by the Committee on Publications may also be published.

5. Communications which have been published elsewhere, so as to be generally accessible, will appear in the Bulletin by title only, but with a reference to the place of publication, if made known in season to the Committee on Publications.

NOTE. *The attention of members to the above rules is specially requested.*

OFFICERS

OF THE

PHILOSOPHICAL SOCIETY OF WASHINGTON

FOR THE YEAR 1881.

President _____ _____ JOSEPH JANVIER WOODWARD.

Vice-Presidents _____ J. K. BARNES,   W. B. TAYLOR,

      J. E. HILGARD,   J. C. WELLING.

Treasurer _____ _____ CLEVELAND ABBE.

Secretaries _____ _____ C. E. DUTTON,   T. N. GILL.

MEMBERS OF THE GENERAL COMMITTEE.

THOMAS ANTISELL,   GARRICK MALLERY,

JOHN R. EASTMAN,   SIMON NEWCOMB,

E. B. ELLIOTT,   JOHN W. POWELL,

WILLIAM HARKNESS,   CHARLES A. SCHOTT.

JOSEPH M. TONER,

STANDING COMMITTEES.

On Communications:

C. E. DUTTON,   GARRICK MALLERY.

On Publications:

S. F. BAIRD,   T. N. GILL,

C. ABBE,   C. E. DUTTON.

(14)

LIST OF MEMBERS

OF

THE PHILOSOPHICAL SOCIETY OF WASHINGTON,

Corrected to July 18th, 1881.

The names of the Founders of the Society, March 13, 1871, are printed in small capitals; for other members the dates of election are given.

> ℥ indicates a life member by payment of 100 dollars.
>
> * indicates absent from the District of Columbia, and excused from dues until announcing their return.
>
> ** indicates resigned.
>
> ? indicates dropped for non-payment of dues, or nothing known of him.
>
> † indicates deceased.

N. B.—It is scarcely possible for the Treasurer to keep a correct record of those who are absent and excused from paying dues, unless members will keep him duly notified of their removals.

THOMAS ANTISELL.
Cleveland Abbe _____1871, October 29.
Benjamin Alvord ____   _____1872, March 23.
Asa O. Aldis_____1873, March 1.
Sylvanus Thayer Abert_____1875, January 30.
Robert Stanton Avery _____1879, October 11.

SPENCER FULLERTON BAIRD.
JOSEPH K. BARNES.
STEPHEN VINCENT BENÉT.
JOHN SHAW BILLINGS.
Orville Elias Babcock_____1871, June 9.
Henry Hobart Bates_____1871, November 4.
† Theodorus Bailey____ _____1873, March 1.
Thomas W. Bartley _____1873, March 29.
Samuel Clagett Busey _____1874, January 17.

Emil Bessels_____1875, January 16.
George Bancroft _____1875, January 30.
* Lester A. Beardslee_____1875, February 27.
* Rogers Birnie_____1876, March 11.
Marcus Baker_____1876, December 2.
Swan Moses Burnett._____1879, March 29.
Alexander Graham Bell_____1879, March 29.
William Birney_____1879, March 29.
Horatio Chapin Burchard_____1879, May 10.

HORACE CAPRON.
THOMAS LINCOLN CASEY.
† SALMON PORTLAND CHASE.
JOHN HUNTINGTON CRANE COFFIN.
† BENJAMIN FANEUIL CRAIG.
CHARLES HENRY CRANE.
Richard Dominicus Cutts _____1871, April 29.
* Augustus L. Case_____1872, November 16.
Robert Craig_____1873, January 4.
Elliott Coues_____1874, January 17.
Josiah Curtis _____1874, March 28.
John White Chickering_____1874, April 11.
* Frank Wigglesworth Clarke_____1874, April 11.
Edward Clark_____1877, February 24.
Frederick Collins_____1879, October 21.
Thomas Craig_____1879, November 22.
John Henry Comstock_____1880, February 14.
Alexander Smythe Christie _____1880, December 4.

WILLIAM HEALEY DALL.
† ALEXANDER B. DYER.
Clarence Edward Dutton_____1872, January 27.
† Richard Crain Dean _____1872, April 23.
Henry Harrison Chase Dunwoody _____1873, December 20.
† Charles Henry Davis_____1874, January 17.
† Frederic William Dorr_____1874, January 17.
Myrick Hascall Doolittle_____1876, February 12.
** George Dewey_____1879, February 15.
Charles Henry Davis _____1880, June 19.
Theodore Lewis DeLand_____1880, December 18.
† AMOS BEEBE EATON.
EZEKIEL BROWN ELLIOTT.
** GEORGE H. ELLIOT.
John Robie Eastman _____1871, May 27.
* Stewart Eldredge_____1871, June 9.
Fredric Miller Endlich _____1873, March 1.
? Charles Ewing _____1874, January 17.

* Hugh Ewing------------------------------1874, January 17.
John Eaton-------------------------------1874, May 8.

* ELISHA FOOTE.
William Ferrel --------------------------1872, November 16.
Edgar Frisby ----------------------------1872, November 16.
†John Gray Foster------------------------1873, January 18.
Edward T. Fristoe------------------------1873, March 29.
Robert Fletcher -------------------------1873, April 10.
Edward Jessop Farquhar ------------------1876, February 12.

THEODORE NICHOLAS GILL.
* BENJAMIN FRANKLIN GREEN.
Henry Goodfellow-------------------------1871, November 4.
Grove Karl Gilbert-----------------------1873, June 7.
Leonard Dunnell Gale---------------------1874, January 17.
* James Terry Gardner--------------------1874, January 17.
George Brown Goode ----------------------1874, January 31.
Henry Gannett----------------------------1874, April 11.
* Edward Oziel Graves -------------------1874, April 11.
Edward Miner Gallaudet ------------------1875, February 27.
Francis Vinton Greene -------------------1875, April 10.
Francis Mathews Green--------------------1875, November 9.
Edward Goodfellow -----------------------1875, December 18.
Alexander Young P. Garnett --------------1878, March 16.
* Walter Hayden Graves ------------------1878, May 25.
* Francis Mackall Gunnell ---------------1879, February 1.
Bernard Richardson Green-----------------1879, February 15.
William Whiting Godding------------------1879, March 29.
James Howard Gore------------------------1880, March 14.
* Adolphus W. Greely--------------------1880, June 19.
Albert Leary Gihon----------------------1880, December 18.

ASAPH HALL.
WILLIAM HARKNESS.
FERDINAND VANDEVEER HAYDEN.
†JOSEPH HENRY.
JULIUS ERASMUS HILGARD.
ANDREW ATKINSON HUMPHREYS.
Henry W. Howgate. ----------------------1878, January 18.
* Edward Singleton Holden --------------1878, June 21.
†Isaiah Hanscom-------------------------1873, December 20.
* Edwin Eugene Howell ------------------1874, January 31.
Henry Wetherbee Henshaw ----------------1874, April 11.
David Lowe Huntingdon ------------------1877, December 21.
George William Hill --------------------1879, February 1.

2

* Peter Conover Hains _____1879, February 15.
* Franklin Benjamin Hough _____,_____1879, March 29.
William Henry Holmes_____1879, March 29.
Ferdinand H. Hassler _____1880, May 8.
William B. Hazen____ _____ _____ _____1881.
THORNTON ALEXANDER JENKINS.
William Waring Johnston_____1873, June 21.
* Henry Arundel Lambe Jackson_____1875, January 30.
William Nicolson Jeffers_____ _____1877, February 24.
Arnold Burgess Johnson_____ _____1878, January 19.
Joseph Taber Johnson _____1879, March 29.   ·
Owen James _____ _____1880, January 3.

* Reuel Keith _____ _____1871, October 29.
John Jay Knox _____1874, May 8.
Albert Freeman Africanus King_____1875, January 16.
† Ferdinand Kampf_____1875, December 18.
** Clarence King _____1879, May 10.
Jerome H. Kidder_____1880, May 8.
Charles Evans Kilbourne _____1880, June 19.

† JONATHAN HOMER LANE.
Nathan Smith Lincoln_____1871, May 27.
** Henry H. Lockwood _____1871, October 29.
** Stephen C. Lyford _____1873, January 18.
William Lee_____1874, January 17.
* Edward Phelps Lull _____1875, December 4.
Eben Jenks Loomis _____1880, February 14.

† FIELDING BRADFORD MEEK.
MONTGOMERY CUNNINGHAM MEIGS.
† ALBERT J. MYER.
William Myers _____1871, June 23.
† Oscar A. Mack _____1872, January 27.
William Manuel Mew _____1873, December 20.
† Archibald Robertson Marvine_____1874, January 31.
† James William Milner _____1874, January 31.
Garrick Mallery_____1875, January 30.
Otis Tufton Mason _____1875, January 30.
William McMurtrie _____1876, February 26.
Aniceto Gabriel Menocal _____1877, February 24.
Martin Ferdinand Morris_____ _____1877, February 24.
* Montgomery Meigs_____1877, March 24.
* Joseph Badger Marvin _____1878, May 25.
Fredrick Bauders McGuire_____1879, February 15.
? Clay Macauley _____1880, January 3.

SIMON NEWCOMB.
WALTER LAMB NICHOLSON.
* Charles Henry Nichols _____ 1872, May 4.
Charles Nordhoff _____ 1879, May 10.

† GEORGE ALEXANDER OTIS.
John Walter Osborne _____ 1878, December 7.

JOHN GRUBB PARKE.
PETER PARKER.
* TITIAN RAMSAY PEALE.
† BENJAMIN PIERCE.
Charles Christopher Parry _____ 1871, May 13.
** Carlisle P. Patterson _____ 1871, November 17.
* Charles Sanders Pierce _____ _____ 1873, March 1.
Orlando Metcalf Poe _____ 1873, October 4.
John Wesley Powell _____ 1874, January 17.
** David Dixon Porter _____ 1874, April 11.
* Albert Charles Peale_____ 1874, April 11.
Robert Lawrence Packard _____ 1875, February 27.
Henry Martyn Paul _____ 1877, May 19.
* Henry Smith Pritchett _____ 1879, March 29.
Daniel Webster Prentiss_ _____ 1880, January 3.

* Christopher Raymond Perry Rodgers_____ 1872, March 9.
* Joseph Addison Rogers_____ 1872, March 9.
John Rodgers_____ 1872, November 16.
* Henry Reed Rathbone_____ 1874, January 17.
* Robert Ridgway _____ 1874, January 31.
† John Campbell Riley_____ 1877, May 19.
Charles Valentine Riley _____ 1878, November 9.
William Francis McKnight Ritter_____ 1879, October 21.

BENJAMIN FRANKLIN SANDS.
† GEORGE CHRISTIAN SCHAEFFER.
CHARLES ANTHONY SCHOTT.
WILLIAM TUCUMSEH SHERMAN.
James Hamilton Saville_____ 1871, April 29.
Ainsworth Rand Spofford _____ 1872, January 27.
? Frederic Adolphus Sawyer_____ 1873, October 4.
John Sherman _____ 1874, January 17.
* John Stearns _____ 1874, March 28.
* Ormond Stone _____ _____ 1874, March 28.
? Aaron Nicholas Skinner _____ 1875, February 27.
Samuel Shellabarger _____ 1875, April 10.
David Smith _____ 1876, December 2.
Edwin Smith _____ 1880, October 23.

* Montgomery Sicard ----------------------------1877, February 24.
Henry Robinson Searle --------------------1877, December 21.
Charles Dwight Sigsbee-------- -----------1879, March 1.
John Patten Story ---------------------1880, June 19.

WILLIAM BOWER TAYLOR.
William Calvin Tilden -----------------1871, April 29.
? George Taylor ---------------------------1873, March 1.
Joseph Meredith Toner -----------------1873, June 7.
Almon Harris Thompson -----------------1875, April 10.
William J. Twining--------------------1878, November 23.
David P. Todd------------------------1878, November 23.

**Jacob Kendrick Upton----------------1878, February 2.
Winslow Upton-------------------------1880, December 4.

George Vasey ------------------------1875, June 5.

*JUNIUS B. WHEELER.
JOSEPH JANVIER WOODWARD.
William Maxwell Wood --------------------1871, December 2.
Francis Amasa Walker --------------------1872, January 27.
James Clarke Welling---------------------1872, November 16.
James Ormond Wilson ------------------1873, March 1.
* George M. Wheeler --------------------1873, June 7.
* John Maynard Woodworth----------------1874, January 21.
Allen D. Wilson ---------------------------1874, April 11.
? Charles Warren-------------------------1874, May 8.
* Joseph Wood-------------------- ----1875, January 16.
* Christopher Columbus Wolcott ----------1875, February 27.
Lester Frank Ward ------- ----------------1876, November 18.
Charles Abiathar White---------------- ----1876, December 16.
Zebulon L. White------------------------1880, June 19.
William Crawford Winlock----------------1880, December 4.

† Mordecai Yarnall --------------------------1871, April 29.
Henry Crissey Yarrow --------------------1874, January 31.

Anton Zumbrock------------------------1875, January 30.

BULLETIN

OF THE

PHILOSOPHICAL SOCIETY OF WASHINGTON.

185TH MEETING.   OCTOBER 9, 1880.

The President in the Chair.

The minutes of the last meeting were read and adopted.

The President notified the meeting of the decease of Prof. PEIRCE' whereupon

Mr. ELLIOTT moved the appointment of a committee of three, to be appointed by the Chair, to draft resolutions in accordance with the notice just given and submit the same at the next meeting.

The Chair appointed as Committee: J. E. HILGARD, J. H. C. COFFIN, and WM. FERRELL.

The treasurer notified the meeting that Vol. 3 of the Bulletin had been published, and that a copy would be forwarded to all members not in arrears.

Mr. C. ABBE communicated the first part of a paper on the Aurora Borealis, referring to studies made by him on the appearance of the aurora of April 4, 1874. He spoke of the difficulty which beset the consideration of the explanation of the appearance of the aurora, and especially of obtaining the altitude of the arch. The present modes of measuring the height yield only negative results, as shown by the experiments of Bravais and Martin, using the trigonometrical method. The second mode employs the varying amount of dip at separate localities, using it according to Galles' method, which assumes the dip of the needle to be of the same amount in the upper regions of the air as at the earth's surface, which has not been proved. Mr. Abbe also referred to Gauss' formula for calculating the direction and intensity of magnetism for all localities, and the defects in Galles' method of calculating the

(21)

heights of auroras, and concluded that we should look with doubt upon all results obtained.

Mr. ABBE then alluded to a third method which has been used by Prof. Newton : this method is based on the assumption that the Aurora describes an arc running round the earth in a circle parallel to the region of greatest frequency of the aurora; this method involves too many assumptions to justify its adoption. It seems impossible to obtain harmonious results from observations at one locality compared with another; nor can the results be made to harmonize with the three methods.

Mr. ELLIOTT alluded to a generally accepted belief that auroras exist at variable heights in the atmosphere, and synchronous with its existence disturbance of the magnetic needle occurs and great electric disturbance, shown by the irregular working of telegraphic apparatus. In the high regions of the air the currents encounter much less resistance than at the earth level.

Mr. OSBORNE made remarks on observations made by him on auroras at Melbourne, and on the appearances of the magnetic light in the southern hemisphere.

Mr. POWELL considered that auroras could occasionally appear in the lower strata of the atmosphere, and referred to an observation of his own in which the arch was placed between the observer and a mountain.

Mr. FARQUHAR called attention to the frequent accounts given of the occurence of the aurora at low levels in high latitudes (as in Norway ;) and as regards the direction of the flashing of the rays as proceeding from below upwards or *vice versa*, this might be an error of observation, similar to observations on the direction of currents or direction of electric light or of magnetism.

The President remarked in closing the discussion that more careful and systematic observations were necessary to determine the height and position of the auroral streamers, and to substantiate the conclusion that the same streamers could not be seen by observers a few miles apart. He cited the general fact of auroras being seen in the north and not in the south over wide stretches of latitude, as one which seems to him difficult to explain on any theory that the aurora was a local phenomenon.

The meeting then adjourned.

186TH MEETING.   OCTOBER 23, 1880.

The President in the Chair.

The minutes of last meeting were read and adopted.

The President notified the meeting of the decease of General A. J. MYER, one of the members of the Society.

Dr. TONER moved the appointment of a committee to draft resolutions suitable to the occasion.

Committee appointed : Messrs. J. C. WELLING, CLEVELAND ABBE, GARRICK MALLERY.

The committee appointed at the last meeting of the Society, to report a resolution commemorative of the decease of Prof. PEIRCE, reported as follows :

Resovled, That the Philosophical Society of Washington put on record their appreciation of the eminent services to science rendered by the late Prof. Benjamin Peirce, of Harvard University, some time since Superintendent of the United States Coast Survey, and during that time a member of this Society.   His introduction of the new modes of condensed mathematical thought into celestial mechanics, and his development of new algebraic methods to their uttermost limit, will ever mark him as one of the most powerful mathematicians of our age.

Mr. ALVORD said he had a warm sympathy with this just and appropriate tribute to the memory of Benjamin Peirce.   Though he could say much in admiration of his genius and of his works, he would now only make an allusion to a mathematical discussion in which Prof. Peirce referred to his friend Agassiz, for whom he always expressed a warm regard.

In the spring of 1865 Prof. Peirce invited the speaker to attend the meeting, at Northampton, in August of that year, of the National Academy of Science, at which he expected to read a paper.   On reaching the room was found arranged around the walls about a dozen large drawings to illustrate the " *Path of the Sling*," which was his topic.   He had obtained an equation of this path. The curve exhibiting this path was very simple in his first drawings and very complicated in the last, according to the changes made in the constants entering into the equation, but the law on the equation of the curve remained the same. The last drawings disclosed highly complex and involved curves not unlike the epicycloids.

Prof. PEIRCE said that these drawings had greatly interested Prof. Agassiz, then absent in his voyage around Cape Horn. It was a striking example of the great varieties and possibilities in nature, buried in the same law. These curves, however apparently different, were traced by the use of the same identical equation, and between the examples exhibited by Prof. Peirce of course myriads of intermediate curves existed. It is obvious that the attraction of all this to Agassiz was the anolagy to organisms in botany and in zoology where groups and species obey some common generalization.

A son of Prof. Peirce has stated that this discussion was never printed, and it is feared that a large share of his brilliant original conception will never be published.

Mr. ELLIOTT referred in warm terms to the genial disposition of Prof. Pierce, and to the encouragement always given by him to young investigators, a characteristic by which he was marked.

Mr. ELLIOTT mentioned that he was the fortunate possessor of a presentation copy of the "Linear Associative Algebra" referred to by Prof. Hilgard, a work which could not fail to impress the investigator with respect and admiration for the great genius of the author.

Prof. HILGARD said he would supplement his first characterization of the ideal algebra, and would call that work the exhaustive treatment of a given mode of investigation, a method of research carried to its uttermost limit and completely exhausted.

Mr. ALVORD stated that Prof. Peirce undoubtedly did a good deal to further the cause of astronomical science by obtaining appropriations to test the value of heights on the Union Pacific Railroad for astronomical observations. In August, 1868, at Chicago, the American Association for the Advancement of Science recommended the establishment of an observatory in that region. Prof. Peirce, as Superintendent of the Coast and Geodetic Survey, had observations made at Sherman Station by Prof. C. A. Young, and on the Sierra Nevada by Prof. Davidson. All this paved the way for the endowment and establishment of the Lick Observatory. These experiments led to the conclusion that the atmosphere of California was most favorable to such observations. The more recent tentative observations of Mr. Burnham at Mount Hamilton confirm these views, and give promise of great success at the Lick Observatory.

Prof. ABBE said that while the scientific and public works of Prof. Peirce would always be spoken of with admiration, his social characteristics were equally interesting. Prof. Abbe could never forget the first time he shook hands with the venerable mathematician in 1860, when he felt that there was a bond of union and sympathy between them. Almost the first words he ever heard him utter gave a glimpse of the man himself. He had heard Prof. Peirce say that the true poet—he who writes the most elevated poetry—is the pure mathematician.

Remarks by Mr. EDWARD GOODFELLOW.

It was my privilege, more than a quarter of a century ago to be ordered to duty under Prof. Peirce's direction, to aid him in certain investigations he was making in behalf of the Coast Survey, with the object of ascertaining the most probable value to be assigned to observations of moon culminations in the determination of differences of longitude.

He was then in the prime of life and upon the threshold of that great fame which his works brought to him but a few years later. He impressed me as a man of thorough kindliness of heart. I came to Cambridge an entire stranger; he interested himself personally in obtaining for me home-like lodgings, and not unfrequently would come to my room to explain in detail, or to write out at length, formulæ which in his own very concise forms had been to me an entire puzzle.

Among the Harvard students he was very popular; his textbooks though were less liked than himself. It was a common saying among the collegians, that Prof. Peirce took for granted, in his books, that every one had as clear an insight into mathematics as he himself had.

I was on duty at West Hills, one of the Coast Survey stations on Long Island, in 1865, when Prof. Peirce came to see Mr. Bache, then just returned from Europe, but not with improved health.

Two years later, the death of Prof. Bache created a great vacancy. At that time the character and qualifications of the man who should succeed him in that high office were thoroughly understood. A recognized pre-eminence among scientific men, an ability to form an independent judgment respecting the problems of geodesy involved in the work—these were essentials. It is enough to say of Prof. Peirce that his appointment amply fulfilled these requirements. Foremost among the geometers of his own land, and regarded as in the front rank of foreign mathematicians, Prof. Peirce, during the first years of his superintendency, developed an administrative ability, which, in the methods of its exercise, won for him the friendly regard and respect of both the older and younger officers of the survey. Recognizing, with a fine tact and courtesy, the conditions entailed upon officers engaged in field work—much physical hardship, small pay, and slow promotion— he established a system of gradual increase of pay at certain intervals, and according to merit.

With Government officials, members of Congress, and all whom it was necessary to consult in obtaining appropriations for the survey, Prof. Peirce was never at fault; he knew how to use the legitimate methods of success; and he will long be remembered, not only as a great mathematician, but as the able director of an important national work.

President NEWCOMB said, as one who had known Prof. Peirce only a little less than a quarter of a century, it might not be inappropriate for him to say a few words, although much that he would have said had been anticipated by those who had already addressed the Society.

One of the most interesting points in Prof. Peirce's character was the fact that he was anything but a mathematician, as conventionally understood—cold, unsympathizing, living in an atmosphere above the rest of the world. Prof. Newcomb had never known any one who had a better heart.

Several members had spoken of the encouragement given by Prof. Peirce to those who first entered upon their life career. The speaker's first interview with that distinguished mathematician had been indelibly impressed upon his mind. What struck him most forcibly about Prof. Peirce at that time was the perfectly unsophisticated way in which he put one at ease, and the total freedom from anything like dignity or pretentiousness which one might suppose would be seen in so great a man.   An interesting trait in Prof. Peirce's intellectual character was his disposition to look at the philosophical side of things.   Altogether, his mathematical works were as much treatises on formal logic as they were on formal mathematics.   The paper on multiple algebra, referred to by Prof. Hilgard, had very much of that character.

Prof. Peirce's method of judging men was peculiar.   Among his students he recognized only two classes—those who knew and those who did not know.   Owing to the general vivacity of his character he invested the driest subjects with interest.   Those who listened to his elocution almost fancied that they understood the highest things he talked about.

Mr. LESTER F. WARD made a communication on the

ANIMAL POPULATION OF THE GLOBE.

He stated that he had recently had occasion to compile, chiefly from official sources, the statistics of live stock in the various countries of the globe from which any data could be obtained, and thought that some of the general results arrived at might possess sufficient scientific interest to warrant laying them before the Society.

The whole number of countries from which information of this character had been collated was twenty-seven, embracing all the countries of Europe except European Turkey, the several British Colonies in Australasia, the Island of Ceylon, Cape Colony and Natal in South Africa, Mauritius, the Dominion of Canada, Newfoundland, Jamaica, the Argentine Republic, Uruguay, Chili, and the United States.   The species of animals of which cognizance was alone taken were: horses, mules, asses, horned cattle, sheep, goats, hogs, buffaloes, and reindeer.   The reports were very incomplete except with respect to the four leading species, viz: horses, cattle, sheep, and hogs.

The total number of each species actually reported upon was as follows :

Horses	47,181,384
Mules	3,474,391
Asses	2,217,166
Mules and asses, not distinguished	11,849

Horned cattle - - - -	157,598,521
Sheep - - - - - -	382,763,015
Goats - - - - - -	15,704,911
Hogs - - - - - -	81,691,331
Buffaloes - - - - -	89,281
Reindeer - - - - -	96,567
	690,828,416

The only species for which an estimate had been made of the total number in the world was the sheep. Mr. Robert P. Porter had made such an estimate, which, though varying from the official data in many of the above countries, afforded a basis for extending the figures already obtained to the remaining portions of the globe, and according to which the ovine population of the earth would reach 577,763,015. Using this result as a basis, a very rough estimate of the number of each of the remaining species in regions not already covered by actual enumerations would place the aggregate number of all the species named throughout the world at a little upward of one billion head and their distribution would then be about as follows:

Horses - - - - - -	70,770,597
Cattle - - - - - -	236,397,781
Sheep - - - - - -	577,763,015
Hogs - - - - - -	100,000,000
All other animals - - - -	32,391,247
	1,017,322,640

Reasons were, however, given for regarding this estimate considerably too low, both as to the number of sheep, upon which it is based, and also in the aggregate, and the speaker thought that the latter would probably reach nearly a billion and a half.

Comparisons were then made with the human population. According to a recent work by Baron Kolb the population of the 27 countries, from which reports were obtained, amounted, in 1878, to 366,100,000. This would give, upon an average, in all these countries, 130 horses, 430 cattle, 1,046 sheep, 224 hogs, and 29 of all the remaining animals taken together, to each 1,000 human beings, and for all these species combined, 1,887 animals to each 1,000 of population.

The latest issue of Behm & Wagner's *Bevölkerung der Erde*, (No. 6,) gives the present population of the earth at 1,456,000,000. If the above estimates of the number of each of these classes of animals in the entire world could be relied upon, they would show, for each 1,000 of human population, 50 horses, 166 cattle, 407 sheep, 70 hogs, and 23 of the other species taken together, or 716 of all the kinds enumerated. But, as above stated, these figures are probably far too low, and, if the truth could be known, it would probably be found that the animal population within these limits would not fall far below the human population.

The paper was concluded with some general observations on the moral bearings of the question of animal domestication. It was held that these facts constituted a sufficient justification of man's general treatment of the brute creation; that a larger amount of animal life exists under man's influence than could exist without it; that he creates more life than he destroys; that his methods of destruction are less painful than those of Nature; that it is to his interest to treat animals well, to supply them with abundant food, and relieve them from those constant fears, both of enemies and of want, which characterize their condition in a wild state; and that when life is taken, it is done quickly and as painlessly as possible; that the reverse of all this is the case in Nature, and hence a great amount of human sympathy is wasted on the creatures under man's control in consequence of ignorance of a few facts and principles.

Observations on the foregoing paper were made by Messrs. ELLIOTT and GILL.

The meeting then adjourned.

187TH MEETING.   10TH ANNUAL MEETING, NOVEMBER 6TH, 1880.

Vice-President HILGARD in the Chair.

Thirty-nine members present.

Meeting called to order by the Chair.

The Secretary read proceedings of the last annual meeting (168th meeting) held November 16th, 1879.

The names of members elected since the last annual meeting were announced.

Preliminary to voting, the list of paid up members was read.

The election of officers for the ensuing year was conducted in accordance with the rules of the Society, with the following results :—

President,	JOSEPH JANVIER WOODWARD.
Vice-Presidents,	W. B. TAYLOR, J. C. WELLING,
	J. E. HILGARD, J. K. BARNES,
Treasurer,	CLEVELAND ABBE.
Secretaries,	T. N. GILL, C. E. DUTTON.

MEMBERS OF THE GENERAL COMMITTEE.

JOHN W. POWELL,	SIMON NEWCOMB,
WILLIAM HARKNESS,	E. B. ELLIOTT,
GARRICK MALLERY,	CHAS. A. SHOTT,
JOHN R. EASTMAN,	THOMAS ANTISELL,

JOS. M. TONER.

It was moved by Mr. COFFIN—

That the consideration of the subject of annual reports to be made by the officers of the Society, be referred to the General Committee, for such action as they may deem desirable.

Adopted.

It was also moved by Mr. COFFIN—

That the General Committee be requested to provide some means for obtaining an annual address from the retiring President and report the same to the Society.

Adopted.

Society then adjourned.

188TH MEETING.   NOVEMBER 20, 1880.

The President, Mr. J. J. WOODWARD, in the Chair, and 58 members present.

The newly-elected President addressed a few remarks to the Society, expressive of his high appreciation of the honor conferred upon him by his election as President of the Society, and conveying assurance of his desire and earnest efforts to fill the office acceptably, and to aid in rendering its meetings interesting and instructive.

The Chair announced the appointment of a Committee on Communications, viz: Mr. C. E. DUTTON and Mr. GARRICK MALLERY.

Mr. J. C. WELLING then presented, pursuant to a resolution of the Society passed at its 186th meeting, the following preamble and resolution relative to the decease of an honored fellow member, viz., the late General ALBERT J. MYER:

WHEREAS in the death of Brigadier General ALBERT J. MYER, late Chief Signal Officer of the Army, this Society has been called upon to mourn the loss of one of its founders as well as one of its most distinguished members, therefore, be it

Resolved, That in testifying our deep regret at the sudden termination of the useful life of General MYER, while as yet he was apparently in the mid-career of his activity, we, at the same time, would record our admiration of those energetic qualities which he brought to every sphere of duty he was called to fill, and by virtue of which he was able, on the one hand, to organize a system of military signaling highly valuable to the Government in the late war, and, on the other hand, to develop a wide field of usefulness by directing the whole energy of the signal service to the study and the practical applications of the science of meteorology, in both which provinces he displayed a remarkable talent for control and great liberality of public spirit.

Resolved, That these proceedings be entered upon the minutes of the Society.

The first communication of the evening was by Mr. JOHN JAY KNOX, entitled

THE DISTRIBUTION OF LOANS IN THE BANK OF FRANCE, THE NATIONAL BANKS OF THE UNITED STATES, AND THE IMPERIAL DANK OF GERMANY.

Mr. KNOX first gave a brief outline of the operations of the Bank of France during and since the late Franco-Prussian war. While it appears that the bank deals in very large amounts of money, particular attention was drawn to the fact that it also distributes among the people smaller amounts than the smallest banks in this country, and, in its annual reports of its transactions, prides itself upon the fact that it has rendered services to so many of the humblest citizens. After reciting the amount of commercial paper discounted, the amount of advances on collateral securities, and the amount of securities of the French Government held by it, he proceeded to quote from the bank reports of 1879 the classification of the Paris bills received at the bank:

Bills of 10 fr., or $2 each, and under   -   -   7,842
Bills of 11 fr. to 50 fr. each, or $2.20 to $10,   392,845
Bills of 51 fr. to 100 fr. each, or $10.20 to $20,   623,232
Bills of above 100 fr. each, or $20   -   -   2,878,294
                                                   ──────────
        Total   -   -   -   -   -   -   3,902,213

The average value of the bills thus discounted at Paris, in 1879, was 859 francs or $171.80. At the branches of the bank, of which there are ninety, the average amount of the bills discounted was 992 francs or $198.40. Similarly in the year 1878, this average value was, at Paris, 892 francs or $178.40, and in the branches of the bank 992 francs or 198.40. The averages for both the bank and its branches were for 1878, 944 francs or $188.80, and for 1879, 900 francs or $180.00.

The bank of France receives these bills from bankers who keep accounts with it as it discounts only for its depositors. These bankers in turn discount them for small brokers who receive them for this purpose from the working classes. The bills are presented at the bank with accompanying schedules. The rate of interest is the same on small bills as on large ones, and no charge is made beyond this ordinary discount or interest. The greater part of these small bills are promissory notes and issued from small manufacturers, and also from workmen on their own account, known as makers of the *Articles de Paris*. The annual exports of such articles amount it is said to twenty-five millions of dollars, and they consist of nic-nacs, toys, dolls, cheap bronze jewelry, and similar products.

Mr. KNOX also gave a classification of the notes and bills discounted and held by the National Banks of the United States on October, 2. 1879, when the total amount of loans was $875,013,107.

Geographical Divisions.	Number of banks.	$100 and less.	Over $100 and less than $500.	$500 and over, but less than $1,000.	$1,000 and over, but less than $5,000.	$5,000 and over, but less than $10,000.	$10,000 and over.	Total.	Amount.	Average.
New England States	547	30,167	54,965	20,444	33,621	10,082	4,590	153,869	$240,552,893 63	$1,563 36
Middle States	641	115,235	132,032	39,484	50,854	11,453	5,276	354,384	416,600,226 30	1,175 56
Southern States	175	15,752	24,480	7,862	8,936	1,283	416	58,729	45,890,807 95	781 40
Western States and Territories	685	90,141	81,563	27,590	31,812	5,381	1,800	241,287	171,969,179 22	712 72
United States	2,048	251,345	296,040	95,382	125,223	28,199	12,081	808,269	$875,013,107 10	$1,082 58

The number of pieces of paper discounted, as will be seen, was 808,269, and the average of each discount, $1,082,59. If the averrage time of these bills was sixty days, and the banks held continually the same amount, the number of discounts made during the year would be nearly five millions (4,849,614), the total discounts more than five thousand millions (5,250,000,000), which would be equal to a discount of $700 annually for each voter, or $500 for each family in the country. The number of notes and bills of $100 each or less at the date named was 251,345, or nearly one-third of the whole; the number of bills of less than $500 each was 547,385, or considerably more than two-thirds of the whole; while the number of bills of less than $1,000 each was 642,765, which is more than three-fourths of the whole number.

Among the States having the smallest average loans were the following: New York, exclusive of the cities of New York and Albany, $499; Pennsylvania, exclusive of Philadelphia and Pittsburgh, $566; Maryland, exclusive of Baltimore, $505; Kansas, in which the average was $353; Iowa, with an average of $375; West Virginia, of $350; Delaware, $556; New Jersey, $566; Minnesota, $621; Vermont, $645; North Carolina, $667; Tennessee, $651; Maine, $740; Indiana, $711; New Hampshire, $815; South Carolina, $846; Georgia, $882.

The Imperial Bank of Germany has a capital of $30,000,000, and is located in the city of Berlin.

The total number of bills of all kinds discounted during the year 1879 was 2,374,394, amounting to $852,175,650; the average amount of each bill being $358.90. The bills are classified as follows: There were 533,564 town bills, amounting to $263,663,280— average $494.15 each; the number of bills on places in Germany was 1,834,351, amounting to $578,693,335, and averaging $315.47 each; and the number of foreign bills was 6,479, in amount $9,819,035, and averaging $1,515.52 each. The average amount of loans and discounts for the year was $82,073,500.

Mr. E. B. ELLIOTT inquired whether it is desirable that bills of such small amounts as those discounted by the Bank of France should be discounted in this country; if so, what plan could be suggested?

Mr. KNOX replied that the savings banks, which receive deposits from all classes and in small amounts, might make small loans.

The laws restrict their investments to the best classes of securities. If there is any class oppressed by the want of loans it is poor people. They have a little money or negotiable property laid aside, upon which they frequently want to borrow, but they find nobody willing to loan upon it. Their only resource is to go to the note shavers and curbstone brokers, who charge them an exorbitant interest. Their wants, in his opinion, could be met by the savings banks.

Mr. J. J. WOODWARD read a communication entitled

RIDDELL'S BINOCULAR MICROSCOPES.—AN HISTORICAL NOTICE,

which is printed in full in the American Monthly Microscopical Journal for December, 1880.

[Abstract.]

Mr. WOODWARD exhibited a large binocular microscope, which he stated had been made for the late Dr. J. L. Riddell, then Professor of Chemistry in the University of Louisiana, during the winter of 1853–4 by the Grunow Brothers, of New Haven, Connecticut, and presented to the Army Medical Museum in April, 1879, by Dr. Riddell's widow.

He said that, although the proper merit of Riddell as a discoverer in this connection had been duly acknowledged by such high continental authorities as Harting and Frey, and even by some English writers, it had been strangely ignored by others, and that even so fair and usually so accurate an author as Dr. Wm. B. Carpenter had fallen into the error of asserting that " the first really satisfactory solution of the problem was that worked out by M. Nachet ;" an error the more remarkable in view of the manner in which Riddell's discovery was published and discussed in England, and of the manner in which it had been used by the opticians of that country.

Mr. WOODWARD then offered evidence to show that Riddell was the first to discover and publish the optical principle on which all the really satisfactory binocular microscopes made prior to the present year depend, as well as the inventor of two efficient and still much employed methods of applying that principle ; one suitable for the simple or dissecting microscope, the other for the compound microscope.

Riddell's discovery was, briefly, that the cone of rays proceeding from a single objective may be so divided by means of reflecting prisms, placed as close behind the posterior combination of the objective as possible, that orthoscopic binocular vision can be obtained both with the simple and the compound microscope. This discov. ery, together with an account of one method of carrying it out, and a suggestion of the feasibility of other methods, was published by Riddell in the New Orleans Mouthly Medical Register for October, 1852, p. 4, and subsequently in the American Journal of Science and Arts, for January, 1853, p. 68. This article was reprinted in London, in the Quarterly Journal of Microscopical Science for April 1853. (Vol. I, 1853, p. 236.)

The contrivance described in this first paper was found by Riddell to give orthoscopic binocular vision when used without eye-pieces, but when ordinary eye-pieces were employed a pseudoscopic effect was obtained. This he obviated by the use of erecting eye-pieces; but, soon after his first paper was published, Riddell devised a second plan, which gave orthoscopic binocular vision with ordinary eye-pieces, and which he subsequently always used for the compound microscope, reserving his first plan for the dissecting (simple) microscope.

A brief notice, containing, however, a correct description of Riddell's second plan, was published in the New Orleans Monthly Medical Register for April, 1853, (p. 78,) and reprinted in London in the Quarterly Journal of Microscopical Science, Vol. I, 1853, (p. 304.) Subsequently, July 30, 1853, Riddell exhibited a dissecting (simple) microscope on his old plan and a compound microscope on his new plan to the American Association for the Advancement of Science, and read a paper describing those instruments, and pretty fully discussing the principles involved. This paper was published in the Proceedings of the Association, Vol. VII, for 1853, (p. 16,) and in the New Orleans Medical and Surgical Journal for November, 1853, (p. 321.) It was reprinted in London in the Quarterly Journal of Microscopical Science for January, 1854, Vol. II, (p. 18.)

Mr. WOODWARD then related the manner in which Riddell's discovery was discussed at the time, in England, by Messrs. Wheatstone and Wenham, and on the continent by M. M. Harting and Nachet. He showed that Nachet's modification of the compound microscope was suggested by Riddell's first instrument, and that Nachet's excellent binocular dissecting (simple) microscope is, in its optical parts, a literal copy of the binocular dissecting (simple) microscope exhibited by Riddell at the Cleveland meeting in July,

1853. This is also true of the binocular dissecting microscopes made of late years by Beck, of London, while the highly lauded erecting binocular microscope of Mr. J. W. Stephenson, F. R. M. S., (1870-72,) is, in its optical parts, a copy of the binocular compound microscope exhibited by Riddell at the Cleveland meeting. The latter instrument, as then exhibited, although optically efficient, was roughly put together by Riddell's own hands. The instrument exhibited by Mr. Woodward was ordered by Riddell of the Grunow Brothers, in August, 1853, and delivered to him by them in March following. In its optical parts it is a copy of the model exhibited at the Cleveland meeting, but some improvements were made in the mechanical details of its construction.

J. S. BILLINGS then made some remarks upon

THE SCIENTIFIC WORK CARRIED ON UNDER THE DIRECTION OF THE NATIONAL BOARD OF HEALTH.

Prof. Ira Remsen, of the Johns Hopkins University, has made for the Board an investigation on the organic matter in the air. By the use of tubes, filled with prepared pumice stone, all the nitrogenous matter in the air to be examined, was removed, and its quantity determined by the usual tests for free and albuminoid ammonia.

Air contaminated by being drawn through water containing decaying meat does not yield more than the usual quantity of albuminoid ammonia.

Air contaminated by being drawn over comparatively dry decaying organic matter yields more than the usual quantity of albuminoid ammonia.

Air contaminated by respiration yields more than the usual quantity of albuminoid ammonia.

The simple statement of fact that a given sample of air yields an abnormally large quantity of albuminoid ammonia is not sufficient to enable us to draw a conclusion with reference to the purity of the air. We must know at what season of the year the air was collected, and whether in the city or country; in fact, we should know everything possible concerning the air, and then let the conclusion finally drawn be a resultant of all the facts. It is probable, however, from what is now known, that the determination of the amount of albuminoid ammonia yielded by air may, under many circumstances, furnish us with important information concerning the quality of the air, but great caution is necessary in dealing with this principle of examination.

A series of investigations upon the effects of various soils upon ordinary sewage has been carried on under the direction of Prof. Pumpelly, of the United States Geological Survey, assisted by Prof. Smythe. The preliminary experiments related to the removal of living organisms from air and fluids by passing these through filters of various kinds, and then testing their effects upon solutions containing organic matter and susceptible of fermentative or putrefactive changes. A very large number of such solutions have been prepared and preserved under various conditions, and in no case has anything like fermentation or the development of the lower organisms been observed, unless under circumstances where the lower organisms could be introduced from without, thus giving strong negative evidence against the theory of spontaneous generation. The filtration of air from such germs was found to be a comparatively easy matter. Passing it through an inch of fine sand deprived it of the power of producing fermentative changes. On the other hand, the removal of bacteroidal organisms from water was much more difficult, filtration through many feet of fine sand being insufficient to effect it. The results reported by Wernich are confirmed, viz., that air passing over putrefying fluids or moist putrefying surfaces does not take up organisms therefrom, nor does it become contaminated by passing over dried bacteria films on smooth compact surfaces such as glass or iron. From woven stuffs, however, it is readily contaminated, and wherever there is dust there is danger.

The results obtained by Dr. Bigelow in attempting to destroy the vitality of dried bacteria films by means of gaseous disinfectants were then mentioned. It is found that time is an important element in the matter, and that long exposures are necessary to secure complete destruction of vitality of such organisms. This may explain the failures to disinfect the Plymouth and the Excelsior by gaseous disinfectants.

Drs. H. C. Wood and H. F. Fremont have made a number of experiments on the inoculation of diphtheria on the lower animals with negative results. The theory of Oertel that this disease is due to specific bacteria is not confirmed by their observations. They state that their results seem to indicate that the contageous material of diphtheria is of the nature of a septic poison which is locally very irritating to the mucous membrane, and that the disease may be often a purely local affection to be treated by local remedies.

Dr. G. M. Sternberg has been repeating the experiments of Klebs and Tommasi-Crudelli on the bacillus malariæ. He finds in the malarious swamps around New Orleans, organisms not distinguishable from those figured by the authors referred to, and on cultivating them in gelatin solutions obtains a similar bacillus. He has not however obtained any specific effects by injecting these organisms into the blood of animals and is unable to confirm the conclusions announced by Klebs.

Dr. Chas. Smart, U. S. A., has been engaged on water analysis, and for the last seven months on the adulterations of food. From an analysis of over six hundred samples he concludes that while there is a considerable amount of adulteration in such articles as ground coffee and spices there is not much that is dangerous to health—in the words of the last British Parliamentary Commission we are cheated but not poisoned. Poisonous colors derived from lead and antimony are found in some candies.

The educational work of the Board was then referred to, and more especially its efforts to secure a uniform and satisfactory mode of reporting mortality statistics.

At the conclusion of Mr. Billings' remarks the society adjourned.

189TH MEETING   DECEMBER 4, 1880.

The President in the chair.

Forty-eight members present.

The minutes of the last meeting were read and adopted.

The Chair announced to the Society the election and acceptance of the following new members: ALEXANDER SMYTHE CHRISTIE, WILLIAM CRAWFORD WINLOCK, and WINSLOW UPTON.

The Chair also announced the appointment of Mr. WILLIAM HARKNESS as an additional member of the Standing Committee on Communications.

The Society then listened to the address of the retiring President, Mr. SIMON NEWCOMB, on

THE RELATION OF SCIENTIFIC METHOD TO SOCIAL PROGRESS.

AMONG those subjects which are not always correctly appre-hended, even by educated men, we may place that of the true significance of scientific method, and the relations of such method to practical affairs. This is especially apt to be the case in a country like our own, where the points of contact between the scientific world on the one hand, and the industrial and political world on the other, are fewer than in other civilized countries. The form which this misapprehension usually takes is that of a failure to appreciate the character of scientific method, and es-pecially its analogy to the methods of practical life. In the judg-ment of the ordinary intelligent man there is a wide distinction between theoretical and practical science. The latter he considers as that science directly applicable to the building of railroads, the construction of engines, the invention of new machinery, the con-struction of maps, and other useful objects. The former he con-siders analogous to those philosophic speculations in which men have indulged in all ages without leading to any result which he considers practical. That our knowledge of nature is increased by its prosecution is a fact of which he is quite conscious, but he considers it as terminating with a mere increase of knowledge, and not as having in its method anything which a person devoted to material interests can be expected to appreciate.

This view is strengthened by the spirit with which he sees scientific investigation prosecuted. It is well understood on all sides that when such investigations are pursued in a spirit really recognized as scientific, no merely utilitarian object is had in view. Indeed it is easy to see how the very fact of pursuing such an object would detract from that thoroughness of examination which is the first condition of a real advance. True science demands in its every research a completeness far beyond what is apparently necessary for its practical applications. The precision with which the astronomer seeks to measure the heavens, and the chemist to determine the relations of the ultimate molecules of matter has no limit, except that set by the imperfections of the instruments of research. There is no such division recognized as that of useful and useless knowledge. The ultimate aim is nothing less than that of bringing all the phenomena of nature under laws as exact as those which govern the planetary motions.

Now the pursuit of any high object in this spirit commands from men of wide views that respect which is felt towards all exertion having in view more elevated objects than the pursuit of gain. Accordingly it is very natural to classify scientists, and philosophers with the men who in all ages have sought after learning instead of utility. But there is another aspect of the question which will show the relations of scientific advance to the practical affairs of life in a different light. I make bold to say that the greatest want of the day, from a purely practical point of view, is the more general introduction of the scientific method and the scientific spirit into the discussion of those political and social problems which we encounter on our road to a higher plane of public well being. Far from using methods too refined for practical purposes, what most distinguishes scientific from other thought is the introduction of the methods of practical life into the discussion of abstract general problems. A single instance will illustrate the lesson I wish to enforce.

The question of the tariff is, from a practical point of view, one of the most important with which our legislators will have to deal during the next few years. The widest diversity of opinion exists as to the best policy to be pursued in collecting a revenue from imports. Opposing interests contend against each other without any common basis of fact or principle on which a conclusion can be reached. The opinions of intelligent men differ almost as widely as those of the men who are immediately interested. But all will admit that public action in this direction should be dictated by one guiding principle—that the greatest good of the community is to be sought after. That policy is the best which will most promote this good. Nor is there any serious difference of opinion as to the nature of the good to be had in view; it is in a word the increase of the national wealth and prosperity. The question on which opinions fundamentally differ is that of the effects of a higher or lower rate of duty upon the interests of the public. If it were possible to foresee, with an approach to certainty, what effect a given tariff would have upon the producers and consumers of an article taxed, and, indirectly, upon each member of the community in any way interested in the article, we should then have an exact datum which we do not now possess for reaching a conclusion. If some superhuman authority, speaking with the voice of infallibility, could give us this information, it is evident that a great national want would be supplied. No question in practical life is more important than this: How can this desirable knowledge of the economic effects of a tariff be obtained?

The answer to this question is clear and simple. The subject must be studied in the same spirit, and, to a certain extent, by the same methods which have been so successful in advancing our knowledge of nature. Every one knows that, within the last two centuries, a method of studying the course of nature has been introduced which has been so successful in enabling us to trace the sequence of cause and effect as almost to revolutionize society. The very fact that scientific method has been so successful here leads to the belief that it might be equally successful in other departments of inquiry.

The same remarks will apply to the questions connected with banking and currency; the standard of value; and, indeed, all subjects which have a financial bearing. On every such question we see wide differences of opinion without any common basis to rest upon.

It may be said, in reply, that in these cases there are really no grounds for forming an opinion, and that the contests which arise over them are merely those between conflicting interests. But this claim is not at all consonant with the form which we see the discussion assume. Nearly every one has a decided opinion on these several subjects; whereas, if there were no data for forming an opinion, it would be unreasonable to maintain any whatever. Indeed, it is evident that there must be truth somewhere, and the only question that can be open is that of the mode of discovering it. No man imbued with a scientific spirit can claim that such truth is beyond the power of the human intellect. He may doubt his own ability to grasp it, but cannot doubt that by pursuing the proper method and adopting the best means the problem can be solved. It is, in fact, difficult to show why some exact results could not be as certainly reached in economic questions as in those of physical science. It is true that if we pursue the inquiry far enough we shall find more complex conditions to encounter, because the future course of demand and supply enters as an uncertain element. But a remarkable fact to be considered is that the difference of opinion to which we allude does not depend upon different estimates of the future, but upon different views of the most elementary and general principles of the subject. It is as if men were not agreed whether air were elastic or whether the earth turns on its axis. Why is it that while in all subjects of physical science we find a general agreement through a wide range of subjects, and doubt commences only where certainty is not attained, yet when we turn to economic subjects we do not find the beginning of an agreement?

No two answers can be given. It is because the two classes of subjects are investigated by different instruments and in a different spirit. The physicist has an exact nomenclature; uses methods of research well adapted to the objects he has in view; pursues his investigations without being attacked by those who wish for different results; and, above all, pursues them only for the purpose of discovering the truth. In economical questions the case is entirely different. Only in rare cases are they studied without at least the suspicion that the student has a preconceived theory to support. If results are attained which oppose any powerful interest, this interest can hire a competing investigator to bring out a different result. So far as the public can see, one man's result is as good as another's, and thus the object is as far off as ever. We may be sure that until there is an intelligent and rational public, able to distinguish between the speculations of the charlatan and the researches of the investigator, the present state of things will continue. What we want is so wide a diffusion of scientific ideas that there shall be a class of men engaged in studying economical problems for their own sake, and an intelligent public able to judge what they are doing. There must be an improvement in the objects at which they aim in education, and it is now worth while to inquire what that improvement is.

It is not mere instruction in any branch of technical science that is wanted. No knowledge of chemistry, physics, or biology, however extensive, can give the learner much aid in forming a correct opinion of such a question as that of the currency. If we should claim that political economy ought to be more extensively studied, we would be met by the question, which of several conflicting systems shall we teach? What is wanted is not to teach this system or that, but to give such a training that the student shall be able to decide for himself which system is right.

It seems to me that the true educational want is ignored both by those who advocate a classical and those who advocate a scientific education. What is really wanted is to train the intellectual powers, and the question ought to be, what is the best method of doing this? Perhaps it might be found that both of the conflicting methods could be improved upon. The really distinctive features, which we should desire to see introduced, are two in number: the one the scientific spirit; the other the scientific discipline. Although many details may be classified under each of these heads, yet there is one of pre-eminent importance on which we should insist.

The one feature of the scientific spirit which outweighs all others in importance is the love of knowledge for its own sake. If by our system of education we can inculcate this sentiment we shall do what is, from a public point of view, worth more than any amount of technical knowledge, because we shall lay the foundation of all knowledge. So long as men study only what they think is going to be useful their knowledge will be partial and insufficient. I think it is to the constant inculcation of this fact by experience, rather than to any reasoning, that is due the continued appreciation of a liberal education. Every business man knows that a business-college training is of very little account in enabling one to fight the battle of life, and that college bred men have a great advantage even in fields where mere education is a secondary matter. We are accustomed to seeing ridicule thrown upon the questions sometimes asked of candidates for the civil service because the questions refer to subjects of which a knowledge is not essential. The reply to all criticisms of this kind is that there is no one quality which more certainly assures a man's usefulness to society than the propensity to acquire useless knowledge. Most of our citizens take a wide interest in public affairs, else our form of government would be a failure. But it is desirable that their study of public measures should be more critical and take a wider range. It is especially desirable that the conclusions to which they are led should be unaffected by partisan sympathies. The more strongly the love of mere truth is inculcated in their nature the better this end will be attained.

The scientific discipline to which I ask mainly to call your attention consists in training the scholar to the scientific use of language. Although whole volumes may be written on the logic of science there is one general feature of its method which is of fundamental significance. It is that every term which it uses and every proposition which it enunciates has a precise meaning which can be made evident by proper definitions. This general principle of scientific language is much more easily inculcated by example than subject to exact description; but I shall ask leave to add one to several attempts I have made to define it. If I should say that when a statement is made in the language of science the speaker knows what he means, and the hearer either knows it or can be made to know it by proper definitions, and that this community of understanding is frequently not reached in other departments of thought, I might be understood as casting a slur on whole departments of inquiry. Without intending any such slur, I may still say that language and statements are worthy of the name scientific as they approach this standard; and, moreover, that a great deal is said and written which does not fulfill the requirement. The fact that words lose their meaning when removed from the connections in which that meaning has been acquired and put to higher uses, is one which, I think, is rarely recognized. There is nothing in the history of philosophical inquiry more curious than the frequency of interminable disputes on subjects where no agreement can be reached because the opposing parties do not use words in the same sense. That the history of science is not free from this reproach is shown by the fact of the long dispute whether the force of a moving body was proportional to the simple velocity or to its square. Neither of the parties to the dispute thought it worth while to define what they meant by the word "force," and it was at length found that if a definition was agreed upon the seeming difference of opinion would vanish. Perhaps the most striking feature of the case, and one peculiar to a scientific dispute, was that the opposing parties did not differ in their solution of a single mechanical problem. I say this is curious, because the very fact of their agreeing upon every concrete question which could have been presented, ought to have made it clear that some fallacy was lacking in the discussion as to the measure of force. The good effect of a scientific spirit is shown by the fact that this discussion is almost unique in the history of science during the past two centuries, and that scientific men themselves were able to see the fallacy involved, and thus to bring the matter to a conclusion.

If we now turn to the discussions of philosophers, we shall find at least one yet more striking example of the same kind. The question of the freedom of the human will has, I believe, raged for centuries. It cannot yet be said that any conclusion has been reached. Indeed I have heard it admitted by men of high intellectual attainments that the question was insoluble. Now a curious feature of this dispute is that none of the combatants, at least on the affirmative side, have made any serious attempt to define what should be meant by the phrase freedom of the will, except by using such terms as require definition equally with the word freedom itself. It can, I conceive, be made quite clear that the assertion, "The will is free," is one without meaning, until we analyze more fully the different meanings to be attached to the word free. Now this word has a perfectly well-defined signification in every day life. We say that anything is free when it is not subject to external constraint. We also know exactly what we mean when we say that a man is free to do a certain act. We mean that if he chooses to do it there is no external constraint acting to prevent him. In all cases a relation of two things is implied in the word, some active agent or power, and the presence or absence of another constraining agent. Now, when we inquire whether the will itself is free, irrespective of external constraints, the word free no longer has a meaning, because one of the elements implied in it is ignored.

To inquire whether the will itself is free is like inquiring whether fire itself is consumed by the burning, or whether clothing is itself clad. It is not, therefore, at all surprising that both parties have been able to dispute without end, but it is a most astonishing phenomenon of the human intellect that the dispute should go on generation after generation without the parties finding out whether there was really any difference of opinion between them on the subject. I venture to say that if there is any such difference, neither party has ever analyzed the meaning of the words used sufficiently far to show it. The daily experience of every man, from his cradle to his grave, shows that human acts are as much the subject of external causal influences as are the phenomena of nature. To dispute this would be little short of the ludicrous. All that the opponents of freedom, as a class, have ever claimed, is the assertion of a causal connection between the acts of the will, and influences independent of the will. True, propositions of this sort can be expressed in a variety of ways connoting an endless number of more or less objectionable ideas, but this is the substance of the matter.

To suppose that the advocates on the other side meant to take issue on this proposition would be to assume that they did not know what they were saying. The conclusion forced upon us is that though men spend their whole lives in the study of the most elevated department of human thought it does not guard them against the danger of using words without meaning. It would be a mark of ignorance, rather than of penetration, to hastily denounce propositions on subjects we are not well acquainted with because we do not understand their meaning. I do not mean to intimate that philosophy itself is subject to this reproach. When we see a philosophical proposition, couched in terms we do not understand, the most modest and charitable view is to assume that this arises from our lack of knowledge. Nothing is easier than for the ignorant to ridicule the propositions of the learned. And yet, with every reserve, I cannot but feel that the disputes to which I have alluded prove the necessity of bringing scientific precision of language into every demand of thought. If the discussion had been confined to a few, and other philosophers had analyzed the subject, and showed the fictitious character of the discussion, or had pointed out where opinions really might differ, there would be nothing derogatory to philosophers. But the most suggestive circumstance is that although a large proportion of the philosophic writers in recent times have devoted more or less attention to the subject, few, or none, have made even this modest contribution. I speak with some little confidence on this subject, because several years ago I wrote to one of the most acute thinkers of the country, asking if he could find in philosophical literature any terms or definitions expressive of the three different senses in which not only the word freedom, but nearly all words implying freedom were used. His search was in vain.

Nothing of this sort occurs in the practical affairs of life. All terms used in business, however general or abstract, have that well-defined meaning which is the first requisite of the scientific language. Now one important lesson which I wish to inculcate is that the language of science in this respect corresponds to that of business; in that each and every term that is employed has a meaning as well defined as the subject of discussion can admit of. It will be an instructive exercise to inquire what this peculiarity of scientific and business language is. It can be shown that a certain requirement should be fulfilled by all language intended for the discovery of truth, which is fulfilled only by the two classes of language which I have described. It is one of the most common errors of discourse to assume that any common expression which we may use always conveys an idea, no matter what the subject of discourse. The true state of the case can, perhaps, best be seen by beginning at the foundation of things, and examining under what conditions language can really convey ideas.

Suppose thrown among us a person of well-developed intellect, but unacquainted with a single language or word that we use. It is absolutely useless to talk to him, because nothing that we say conveys any meaning to his mind. We can supply him no dictionary, because by hypothesis he knows no language to which we have access. How shall we proceed to communicate our ideas to him? Clearly there is but one possible way, namely, through his five senses. Outside of this means of bringing him in contact with us we can have no communication with him. We, therefore, begin by showing him sensible objects, and letting him understand that certain words which we use correspond to those objects. After he has thus acquired a small vocabulary, we make him understand that other terms refer to relations between objects which he can perceive by his senses. Next he learns, by induction, that there are terms which apply not to special objects, but to whole classes of objects. Continuing the same process, he learns that there are certain attributes of objects made known by the manner in which they affect his senses, to which abstract terms are applied. Having learned all this, we can teach him new words by combining words without exhibiting objects already known. Using these words we can proceed yet further, building up, as it were, a complete language. But there is one limit at every step. Every term which we make known to him must depend ultimately upon terms the meaning of which he has learned from their connection with special objects of sense.

To communicate to him a knowledge of words expressive of mental states it is necessary to assume that his own mind is subject to these states as well as our own, and that we can in some way indicate them by our acts. That the former hypothesis is sufficiently well established can be made evident so long as a consistency of different words and ideas is maintained. If no such consistency of meaning on his part were evident, it might indicate that the operations of his mind were so different from ours that no such communication of ideas was possible. Uncertainty in this respect must arise as soon as we go beyond those mental states which communicate themselves to the senses of others.

We now see that in order to communicate to our foreigner a knowledge of language, we must follow rules similar to those necessary for the stability of a building. The foundation of the building must be well laid upon objects knowable by his five senses. Of course the mind, as well as the external object, may be a factor in determining the ideas which the words are intended to express; but this does not in any manner invalidate the conditions which we impose. Whatever theory we may adopt of the relative part played by the knowing subject, and the external object in the acquirement of knowledge, it remains none the less true that no knowledge of the meaning of a word can be acquired except through the senses, and that the meaning is, therefore, limited by the senses. If we transgress the rule of founding each meaning upon meanings below it, and having the whole ultimately resting upon a sensuous foundation, we at once branch off into sound without sense. We may teach him the use of an extended vocabulary, to the terms of which he may apply ideas of his own, more or less vague, but there will be no way of deciding that he attaches the same meaning to these terms that we do.

What we have shown true of an intelligent foreigner is necessarily true of the growing man. We come into the world without a knowledge of the meaning of words, and can acquire such knowledge only by a process which we have found applicable to the intelligent foreigner. But to confine ourselves within these limits in the use of language requires a course of severe mental discipline. The transgression of the rule will naturally seem to the undisciplined mind a mark of intellectual vigor rather than the reverse. In our system of education every temptation is held out to the learner to transgress the rule by the fluent use of language to which it is doubtful if he himself attaches clear notions, and which he can never be certain suggests to his hearer the ideas which he intends. Indeed, we not infrequently see, even among practical educators, expressions of positive antipathy to scientific precision of language so obviously opposed to good sense that they can be attributed only to a failure to comprehend the meaning of the language which they criticise.

Perhaps the most injurious effect in this direction arises from the natural tendency of the mind, when not subject to a scientific

4

discipline, to think of words expressing sensible objects and their relations as connoting certain supersensuous attributes. This is frequently seen in the repugnance of the metaphysical mind to receive a scientific statement about a matter of fact simply as a matter of fact. This repugnance does not generally arise in respect to the every day matters of life. When we say that the earth is round we state a truth which every one is willing to receive as final. If without denying that the earth was round, one should criticise the statement on the ground that it was not necessarily round but might be of some other form, we should simply smile at this use of language. But when we take a more general statement and assert that the laws of nature are inexorable, and that all phenomona, so far as we can show, occur in obedience to their requirements, we are met with a sort of criticism with which all of us are familiar, and which I am unable adequately to describe. No one denies that as a matter of fact, and as far as his experience extends, these laws do appear to be inexorable. I have never heard of any one professing, during the present generation, to describe a natural phenomenon, with the avowed belief that it was not a product of natural law; yet we constantly hear the scientific view criticised on the ground that events may occur without being subject to natural law. The word "may," in this connection, is one to which we can attach no meaning expressive of a sensuous relation.

This is, however, not the most frequent misuse of the word may. In fact, the unscientific use of language to which I refer, is most strongly shown in disquisitions on the freedom of the will. When I say that it is perfectly certain that I will to-morrow perform a certain act unless some cause external to my mind which I do not now foresee occurs to prevent me, I make a statement which is final so far as scientific ideas are concerned. But it will sometimes be maintained that however certain it may be that I shall perform this act, nevertheless I may act otherwise. All I can say to this is that I do not understand the meaning of the statement.

The analogous conflict between the scientific use of language and the use made by some philosophers, is found in connection with the idea of causation. Fundamentally the word cause is used in scientific language in the same sense as in the language of common life. When we discuss with our neighbors the cause of a fit of illness, of a fire, or of cold weather, not the slightest ambiguity attaches to the use of the word, because whatever meaning may be given to it is founded only on an accurate analysis of the ideas involved in it from daily use. No philosopher objects to the common meaning of the word, yet we frequently find men of eminence in the intellectual world who will not tolerate the scientific man in using the word in this way. In every explanation which he can give to its use they detect ambiguity. They insist that in any proper use of the term the idea of power must be connoted. But what meaning is here attached to the word power, and how shall we first reduce it to a sensible form, and then apply its meaning to the operations of nature? That this can be done, I by no means deny. All I maintain is that if we shall do it, we must pass without the domain of scientific statement.

Perhaps the greatest advantage in the use of symbolic and other mathematical language in scientific investigation is that it cannot possibly be made to connote anything except what the speaker means. It adheres to the subject matter of discourse with a tenacity which no criticism can overcome. In consequence, whenever a science is reduced to a mathematical form its conclusions are no longer the subject of philosophical attack. To secure the same desirable quality in all other scientific language it is necessary to give it, so far as possible, the same simplicity of signification which attaches to mathematical symbols. This is not easy, because we are obliged to use words of ordinary language, and it is impossible to divest them of whatever they may connote to ordinary hearers.

I have thus sought to make it clear that the language of science corresponds to that of ordinary life, and especially of business life, in confining its meaning to phenomena. An analogous statement may be made of the method and objects of scientific investigation. I think Professor Clifford was very happy in defining science as organized common sense. The foundation of its widest general creations is laid, not in any artificial theories, but in the natural beliefs and tendencies of the human mind. Its position against those who deny these generalizations is quite analogous to that taken by the Scottish school of philosophy against the skepticism of Hume.

It may be asked, if the methods and language of science correspond to those of practical life,—why is not the every day discipline of that life as good as the discipline of science? The answer is, that the power of transferring the modes of thought of common life to subjects of a higher order of generality is a rare faculty which can be acquired only by scientific discipline. What we want is that in public affairs men shall reason about questions of finance, trade, national wealth, legislation and administration with the same consciousness of the practical side that they reason about their own interests. When this habit is once acquired and appreciated, the scientific method will naturally be applied to the study of questions of social policy. When a scientific interest is taken in such questions, their boundaries will be extended beyond the utilities immediately involved, and then the last condition of unceasing progress will be complied with.

At the conclusion of **Mr. Newcomb's** address it was moved by **Mr.** Hilgard that the thanks of the Society are due to Mr. Newcomb for his weighty, instructive, and interesting address.

The motion was carried.

Mr. J. E. HILGARD then made a communication on the subject of

A MODEL OF THE BASIN OF THE GULF OF MEXICO.

He exhibited to the Society a model of the Gulf of Mexico recently constructed under the direction of the Coast Survey Office upon data obtained by a very great number of soundings. Of these many thousands have been made, and the model is believed to be very correct. As constructed, the vertical scale is thirty times as great as the horizontal in order to emphasize and render easily intelligible the most notable features.

The soundings of the waters in the Gulf of Mexico began with the extension thither of the work of the Coast Survey, but they were at first only littoral and tributary to the topographic and hydrographic work of the Bureau. They were interrupted by the civil war, but were resumed at its close. Soundings had also been made off the east coast of Florida to ascertain the nature and dimensions of the outlet of the Gulf stream. This outlet was found to be relatively quite small. Soundings and temperatures had been taken from Florida to Cuba and to Yucatan. Within a few years the work of exploring the general configuration of the Gulf of Mexico has been commenced by Commander Sigsbee, of the Navy, on duty in the Coast and Geodetic Survey. This officer made great improvements in deep-sea sounding apparatus, and, prosecuting the exploration with great energy and ingenuity, has brought the work to a speedy conclusion.

As a result of these investigations, it is found that the continental profiles which descend from every direction beneath the water of the gulf, have, at first, a very gradual slope of a few feet to the mile—until the 100 fathom depth, or thereabout, is reached. They then descend much more rapidly, and, in some places, with singular abruptness to depths exceeding 2,000 fathoms. All around the gulf shores is a marginal belt of varying width and of comparatively shallow water. Within this marginal belt is an area of similar shape to that of the gulf itself, and nearly concentric with its coast, where the depth is comparable to that of mid-ocean. The extent of the deeper area is about 50,000 square miles. It also appears that the continental or peninsular mass of Florida is of much greater area than that portion which exposes its surface above the water, and the same is true of Yucatan. An examination of the portions in the vicinity of the Mississippi river, shows that the delta has very nearly reached the position where the profile begins to drop rapidly down into deep water, and the apprehensions of those who fear that the jetties lately constructed may cause the accumulation of deposits further out may therefore be dispelled or greatly mitigated.

Turning to the channel of the Gulf stream, Mr. Hilgard remarked that its transverse section between Florida and the Bahama Banks, did not exceed twelve square miles. With an average current velocity of only $2\frac{1}{2}$ miles per hour, it appears quite incredible that enough water can be dischaged through this passage to occasion the mild climate of western Europe. The main mass of the great oceanic drift which warms these shores, he thought must be derived from the Caribbean Sea, passing out between the greater Antilles, where the passes are far wider and deeper. Of this greater oceanic drift the efflux through the Florida straits forms but a small part.

Remarks upon this communication were made by Messrs. ALVORD, DUTTON, GILL, HARKNESS and WHITE.

The Society then adjourned.

190TH MEETING.   DECEMBER 18, 1880.

The President in the Chair.

Forty-two members present.

The minutes of the last meeting were read and adopted.

A communication was then read by Mr. Swan M. Burnett, entitled

COLOR PERCEPTION AND COLOR BLINDNESS.

The speaker first gave the Young-Helmholtz theory, which consists in the assumption of three fibres in the retina corresponding to the so-called fundamental colors, red, green and violet, stating the objections that have been brought against this theory by Mauthner and others, when viewed from the standpoint of color blindness.

He then explained in brief the theory of Prof. Hering, of Prague, according to which there are supposed to be in the retina three chemical substances, which are called the *black-white*, the *red-green*, and the *blue-yellow*. These are acted on by light, by assimilation, and by dissimilation. Dissimilation (D) of the black-white substance produces white, its assimilation (A) black. The D-action on the red-green produces red, the A-action green. The D-action on the blue-yellow substance produces blue, the A-action yellow. When one of the substances is lacking there is an inability to properly perceive the pair of colors peculiar to it. There is therefore red-green blindness, and blue-yellow blindness. The objections to this theory as advanced by Prof. Donders and others were then brought forward.

There are two strong objections to both these theories aside from those mentioned, first, their want of simplicity, and second, the necessity of inventing new tissues and novel reactions of tissues to the affecting agent.

The true theory of colors, when found, we have every right to expect will be simple, and the laws governing it will be in keeping with the action of light on simple substances, and in the opinion of the speaker, they would be found to lie in the direction of the recent discoveries of the action of light on the molecular structure of homogeneous substances, and he accepted as the foundation of his speculations that *variation in sensation would have its basis, not in complexity of tissue, but in the varying action of the affecting agent.*

A theory on this basis would have the retina a substance whose molecular structure would be such as to allow it to respond promptly to each of those undulations of the ether corresponding to the principal colors. The wave length corresponding to red, for example, would produce a molecular change (most probably simply vibratory) which would be carried to the brain centre of vision by the optic nerve, and there transformed into a distinct sensation.   The same would hold good probably for the orange, yellow, green, blue and violet. We have an analogy for such reaction in the molecular change produced by light in the metal selenium when in a crystallized state, and in some other substances.   The photophone depends for its existence upon this delicate reaction of the molecular structure of selenium to the influence of light.   Which are the primary and which the secondary colors—that is those arising from mixed sensations—would have to be determined by experiment.

The speaker would divide color blindness into two classes, *peripheral* and *central*.   In the former the retina and optic nerve would be the agents affected, in the latter the cerebral centre of vision.   The latter he considered to be the most common form of congenital color blindness, and it was due in his opinion to the fact that this centre had not yet developed the power of properly differentiating the closely allied impressions sent to it.   In such cases, the spectrum was not shortened, but was seen dichromic, the line of demarcation being usually at the blue.

As regards the *retinal* form one broad general principle might be laid down, that where there was a lacking color the molecular changes in the retina were such as to incapacitate it from responding promptly to the wave lengths which physically represent that color.

Believing that education had much to do with the development of the color-sense, the speaker had devised a plan for the " systematic education of the color-sense in children," which, if followed out closely, would, he believed, in the course of generations, make color-blindness as rare in the male sex as it now is among females.   This plan is published in full in the Archives of Ophthalmology.   (G. P. Putnam's Sons, New York, October, 1879.)

The next communication was by Mr. E. M. GALLAUDET, entitled—

THE INTERNATIONAL CONVENTION OF THE TEACHERS OF THE DEAF AND DUMB, AT MILAN.

Mr. GALLAUDET recited first certain resolutions adopted at that convention, which were as follows :

" The convention, considering the incontestable superiority of speech over signs, 1st, for restoring deaf-mutes to social life, 2d, for giving them greater facility of language, declares that the method of articulation should have the preference over that of signs in the instruction and education of the deaf and dumb.

" Considering that the simultaneous use of signs and speech has the disadvantage of injuring speech and lip reading and precision of ideas, the convention declares that the pure oral method ought to be preferred."

Apropos to these resolutions, Mr. GALLAUDET quoted the comments of the London *Times*, which journal remarks that—

" No more representative body could have been collected than that which at Milan has declared for oral teaching for the deaf and dumb, and for nothing but oral teaching," and also speaks of the action of the convention as expressing a " virtual unanimity of preference for oral teaching, which might seem to overbear all possibility of opposition."

Mr. GALLAUDET then proceeded to explain the composition of the convention, which, he stated, consisted of 164 members, of whom eighty-seven were Italians and fifty-six French, these two nationalities composing seven-eighths of its representation. There were from America five members, while the city of Milan alone furnished forty-six. The president and secretary, both oralists, were from Milan, and seven out of eight other officers were also oralists. The Paris convention, in 1878, had been organized by the Pereire Society, an active propaganda in favor of the exclusive oral method ; and the organization of the Milan convention was of a similar nature, and cannot be regarded as representative of the general body of instructors of the deaf and dumb throughout the world, as the preceding statement of its composition must indicate. The American delegates voted in favor of the combined method of teaching, both orally and by signs.

He expressed, in closing, the conviction that teachers of this country are working in the right direction, and that, in due time, the relative importance as well as the proper sphere of the two methods will be fully recognized in the combined system.

191ST MEETING.   JANUARY 8, 1881.

Vice-President TAYLOR in the Chair.

Twenty-seven members present.

The minutes of the last meeting were read and adopted.

A communication by Mr. W. F. McK. RITTER was then read, entitled—

ON A SIMPLE METHOD OF DERIVING SOME EQUATIONS USED IN THE THEORY OF THE MOON AND OF THE PLANETS.

The rectangular and polar co-ordinates of a heavenly body are functions of the elements of the orbit and of the time. When the elements are pure constants, as in the case of undisturbed motion, these co-ordinates vary only with the time; but when the effect of the disturbing force is considered, we have variation or perturbation of the elements, and hence, also, the co-ordinates vary both with the time and the elements.

Since the co-ordinates are functions of the elements, as long as the variations of the elements are unknown, the corresponding corrections to the co-ordinates, due to these variations, must be regarded as zero. Hence, in the differentiation, the differentials of the co-ordinates with respect to the elements, alone considered as variable, must be put equal to zero. Hence, also, the velocities of the rectangular and polar co-ordinates are zero, and thus we are furnished with equations of condition, which greatly facilitate the solution of the problem of determining the perturbations of the elements.

In finding what are called the special perturbations, we resolve the disturbing force into three components.

For this purpose, call

R, the component in the direction of the radius-vector,

S, the component perpendicular to the radius-vector, parallel to the plane of the orbit, and positive in the direction of the motion, and

Z, the component perpendicular to the plane of the orbit.

The values of these components, in the form we wish to employ, are

$$R = k^2 (1 + m) \ \frac{d\,\Omega}{dr},$$

$$S = k^2 \dot{(1} + m) \ \frac{1}{r} \ \frac{d\,\Omega}{dv},$$

$$Z = k^2 (1 + m) \ \frac{d\,\Omega}{dz}.$$

Here Ω is the disturbing function, r and v are polar co-ordinates, z the co-ordinate perpendicular to the plane of the orbit, k^2 the

Gaussian constant, and m the relation of the mass of the disturbed body to that of the sun.

By putting the first differential co-efficients of the co-ordinates with respect to the time equal to zero, we derive, with great ease, the expressions for the variations of the elements. This is for the case of special perturbations. These expressions will contain the components R, S, and Z.

If we now substitute the values of these components, wherever they appear, and perform the necessary reductions, we get expressions for the variations of the elements, where, instead of the components of the disturbing force, the force itself appears.

In the case of the mean anomaly, another method has been followed. Its variation can best be found by means of the relation

$$M = \mu (t - T),$$

where M represents the mean anomaly, μ the mean daily motion, and T the time of perihelion-passage.

I have thus derived, among others, the equations :

$$\frac{dL}{dt} = k^2 (1 + m) \frac{d\Omega}{dM}, \quad \frac{dM}{dt} = - k^2 (1 + m) \frac{d\Omega}{dL}$$

$$\frac{dG}{dt} = k^2 (1 + m) \frac{d\Omega}{d\omega}, \quad \frac{d\omega}{dt} = - k^2 (1 + m) \frac{d\Omega}{dG},$$

$$\frac{dH}{dt} = k^2 (1 + m) \frac{d\Omega}{d\Omega}, \quad \frac{d\Omega}{dt} = - k^2 (1 + m) \frac{d\Omega}{dH}.$$

From these, by slight changes, we get the equations used by Delaunay in his theory of the moon's motion. Thus by putting $k^2 (1 + m) \Omega = R$, and writing l, g, h, for M, ω, Ω, respectively, we have

$$\frac{dL}{dt} = \frac{dR}{dl}, \quad \frac{dl}{dt} = - \frac{dR}{dL},$$

$$\frac{dG}{dt} = \frac{dR}{dg}, \quad \frac{dg}{dt} = - \frac{dR}{dG},$$

$$\frac{dH}{dt} = \frac{dR}{dh}; \quad \frac{dh}{dt} = - \frac{dR}{dH}.$$

In these equations, according to the notation of Delaunay, $L = \sqrt{a\mu}$, μ being the sum of the masses of the earth and moon, $G = L\sqrt{1 - e^2}$, $H = G \cos i$; a, e, and i being the semi-major axis, eccentricity, and inclination respectively; l designates the mean anomaly, g the angular distance of the ascending node from the perigee, and h the longitude of the ascending node.

The equations which Le Verrier uses in his theories of the planets are not as simple in form as those of Delaunay; but there is no difficulty attending their derivation by this method. The method Le Verrier uses in deriving them is long and cumbrous. Delaunay does not stop to derive the equations he uses, but refers, on this head, to a memoir by Benét.

By the method given above I have derived all the fundamental equations used by these authors, and by those who have considered the subject of perturbations from the same standpoint.

I think I have here given enough of the process to enable any one to understand the method. I may add that the method occurred to me seven or eight years ago.

The next communication was by Mr. EDGAR FRISBY

ON THE ORBIT OF SWIFT'S COMET.

This comet was first observed by Prof. Swift of Rochester, October 10, 1880, and was reported by him as moving directly towards the earth. It was observed by Prof. Eastman with the transit circle of the U. S. Naval Observatory on the evenings of October 25, November 7, and November 20, and from the data so obtained the following elements were computed by Prof. Frisby:

Epoch of perihelion passage $7^d.775675$ Washington mean time

$$\left.\begin{array}{rl} \Omega = & 296° \ 48' \ 19.''9 \\ \pi = & 42° \ 59' \ 15.''8 \\ \vartheta = & 42° \ 26' \ 48.''5 \\ \iota = & 5° \ 30' \ 35.''9 \\ \log a = & 0.517002 \\ \log \mu = & 2.774504 \end{array}\right\} \text{Mean Equinox 1880.0.}$$

From these elements it will be inferred that it was moving very nearly towards the earth at the time of discovery, October 10. On November 8, it came very near the earth's orbit, its distance from it then being about 0.069 of the earth's mean distance from the sun. The aphelion lies just beyond Jupiter's orbit so that its perturbations are liable at any time to become immense. The periodic time from the elements is about 2,178 days, or a little less than six years, but Jupiter's position in his orbit is now such that it is not likely to come near the comet for a long period. For a time after the discovery of the comet it was doubtful whether the period was 11 or $5\frac{1}{2}$ years. The latter is undoubtedly the true one, the slight discrepancy being due to insufficient data. It would probably be impossible to see it at every return, for assuming its period to be approximately 5½ years, the earth would at each alternate return be at the opposite side of its orbit, and the sun would then intervene between the earth and the comet. It passed nearest to the earth about the 18th of November.

The logarithms of the radii vectores and distance from the earth on the dates given are:

	log. r	log. Δ
October 25,	0.035328	9.221510
November 7,	0.029018	9.141693
November 20,	0.034557	9.119295

No theory about any periodic time was assumed in these calculations.

At the conclusion of Mr. Frisby's paper the Society adjourned.

192D MEETING.   JANUARY 22, 1881.

The President in the Chair.

Thirty-seven members present.

The following communication was read by Mr. J. W. CHICKERING, entitled—

NOTES ON ROAN MOUNTAIN, NORTH CAROLINA.

The great Appalachian chain, with its undulating line of 1,300 miles, from the promontory of Gaspè, on the Gulf of St. Lawrence, to Georgia and Alabama, beginning as a series of simple folds of moderate height, increases in complexity as in altitude from north to south, attaining its greatest elevation in a veritable mountain knot in the Black range. Following it from its commencement to the Hudson, we find the single chain of the Green Mountains, rising to its extreme height in Mount Mansfield, 4,430 feet, with, on the east, the outlying clusters of the White Mountains in New Hampshire, with Mount Washington reaching 6,288 feet, and others exceeding 5,000 feet, and Mount Katahdin in Maine, 100 miles away, about 5,200 feet, and on the west the Adirondack group, rising to 5,379 feet, and the Catskills considerably lower.

From the Hudson to the New River in Virginia, 450 miles, through the States of New Jersey, Pennsylvania, and Virginia, it gradually gains in both width and altitude, consisting of many parallel ranges, with fertile valleys between, of which the great valley of Virginia is the largest and best known. In Pennsylvania the summits vary from 800 to 2,500 feet. Toward the south the chains become more numerous and in Virginia the Peaks of Otter reach 4,000 feet. The extreme eastern range is called the Blue Ridge, the extreme western the Cumberland Mountains, or, more properly, Plateaus, while the high range or ranges between are, in general, called the Alleghanies.

From the New River south the system becomes much more complex. The main chain, hitherto called the Blue Ridge, is deflected to the west, and for 250 to 300 miles, in a circuitous chain, under the names of Iron, Stone, Bald, Great Smoky, and Unaka Mountains, forms the boundary line between North Carolina and Tennessee, rising frequently to heights exceeding 6,000 feet; while the more easterly range, retaining the name of Blue Ridge, and finding its southern terminus at Cæsar's Head, in South Carolina, where it turns abruptly to the northwest, reaches even loftier altitudes, Mitchell's high peak being accredited with 6,717 feet.

In North Carolina these two ranges are more than 50 miles apart, are partially connected by transverse ranges, and, for more than 100 miles, constitute a great central plateau, like that of Colorado on a small scale.

As says Prof. Guyot, "Here then through an extent of more than 150 miles the mean height of the valley from which the mountains rise is more than 2,000 feet. The mountains which reach 6,000 feet are counted by scores, and the loftiest peaks exceed 6,700 feet, while at the north, in the group of the White Mountains, the base is scarcely 1,000 feet, the gaps 2,000 feet, and Mount Washington, the only one which rises above 6,000 feet, is still 400 feet below the Black Dome of the Black Mountains. Here then, in all respects, is the culminating region of the vast Appalachian system."

The eastern chain, or Blue Ridge is still the watershed, and, on the Atlantic slope, gives birth to the Roanoke, Catawba, Broad, Saluda, and Savannah rivers; while on the other side this area of mountains and plateaus is separated by transverse chains into many deep basins, at the bottom of each one of which runs one of those mountain streams, which are compelled to cut their way to the Tennessee through gaps, gorges, and defiles in the very heart of this mighty chain, giving us some of the most picturesque scenery to be found on the continent. Among these, the New, Watauga, Nolichucky, and French Broad are the best known.

In the midst of this region, with all three ranges in sight, stands Roan Mountain, Laurentian in age, the State line crossing it at an altitude of 6,391 feet, as determined by the mean of my barometrical observations—and on and about this mountain it was my good fortune to stay from June 25th to August 30th.

Notes upon some of the peculiarities of the region, as contrasted with the northern Appalachian, will be my apology for asking your attention.

I. The Uniformity of Elevation.

Standing on the summit of Roan, we look into seven different States, and command a horizon of 30 to 80 miles. On the north and west the eye catches the Cumberland range in the horizon, beyond the great Tennessee plateau, which is traversed by the Clinch and a score of other ranges, but all as level as if designed for railroad embankments.

On the south and east there is a wilderness of mountains. Guyot gives 50 to 60 with altitudes exceeding 6,000 feet, and yet the highest is only 6,717 feet, and perhaps 40 of them fall between 6,000 and 6,500, while hundreds of others are above 5,000. The valleys rarely go below 3,000 feet. The railroad after leaving Lynchburg reaches 1,000 feet in a few miles, and from that point for nearly 300 miles never goes below 1,500 feet, its highest summit being at 2,550 feet.

II. Uniformity of Temperature.

During nine weeks the mercury once indicated 75°, seven times 70° +, once 45°, three times 50°, the general daily variation being between 55° and 65°. The spring, a few rods rods from the hotel, has a temperature of 45°. Equally remarkable was the uniformity of atmospheric pressure the highest barometer being 24.19, and the lowest 23.87, or a difference of only 0.32 inches. No wind had a velocity of more than twenty miles an hour, and seldom did it reach ten.

III. Fertility of the Summit.

Instead of the upper 1,000 feet being, as in most of the northern Appalachian peaks reaching an altitude of over 5,000 feet, a pile of barren rocks, with lichens their only vegetation, the summit of Roan, and many other peaks, is a smooth, grassy slope, of the most vivid green, dotted with clumps of *Alnus viridis*, and *Rhododendron catawbiense*, the soil one or two feet in depth, rich and black. How this amount of humus was accumulated on these summits, and what cause destroyed the forests which its existence would seem to indicate as formerly existing, are questions not easily answered.

The valleys are very fertile, and adapted to almost any crop.

At an elevation of 3,000 to 4,000 feet occurs a belt of the most magnificent forest trees I have ever seen—hundreds of chestnuts, sugar maples, lindens, tulip trees, yellow birches, buck-eyes—some from 4 to 7 feet in diameter, and rising 70 to 80 feet without a limb. One chestnut measured 24 feet in circumference, and one black cherry measured 19 feet. Thorn bushes are as large as old apple trees with dwarf buck-eyes and yellow birches, looked like old orchards of vast extent.

IV. Flora.

Ascending the mountain, the vegetation takes on a northern aspect. Hemlocks abound till near the summit, where they are replaced by *Abies Fraseri*, the characteristic species of these summits.

Anemone nemorosa, Oxalis acetosella, Rubus odoratus, Ribes lacustre and *prostratum, Aster acuminatus, Habenaria articulata, Veratrum viride, Lycopodium lucidulum*, and similar species, remind one of the woods of Maine or New Hampshire.

The peculiar flora of the upper 1,000 feet, greatly resembles in habit that of the White Mountains, but very few species are the same. *Paronychia argyrocoma, Lycopodium selago* and *Alnus viridis*, are almost the only plants that occur to me as identical in the two localities, and these in the White Mountains are found in Crawford Notch, while in Roan they are near the summit. *Arenaria groenlandica* is replaced by *A. glabra, Solidago thyrsoidea* by *S. glomerata ; Geum radiatum* of the North is a variety of that found here ; the two dwarf *Nabali* of White Mountains are represented by a new species, *N. roanensis, Rhododendron lapponicum* (four inches high) by magnificent *R. catawbiense*, covering the summit with its domes of inflorescence six to eight feet in diameter, *Castilleia pallida* by *C. coccinea.*

So that, in general, the species peculiar to these mountains are hardly sub-alpine, and thus continuous with similar species further north, but are rather apparent instances of local variation, many species being confined to very limited localities.

On Mount Washington, a few rods will often give the same plant in bud, flower, and fruit, as a north or south exposure, a precipice, or a snow-drift may retard or accelerate growth; but on these southern mountains no such difference obtains any more than in the valleys below.

On this communication Mr. J. W. POWELL remarked that the uniformity in the altitudes of the peaks is a feature resulting from the fact that the general mass out of which they have been carved by erosion possesses a plateau structure. The elevation of that region was distributed in its effects with an approach to uniformity over a wide extent of country, and was unaccompanied by those sharp flexings or the protrusions of abrupt mountain cores, which are encountered in some portions of the Appalachians and other mountainous regions. The individual masses and ranges in the Cumberland region are the work of erosion—the general process of land sculpture acting upon a broad platform, excavating broad valleys and narrow gorges, and leaving the peaks and ridges as cameos— mere remnants left in the general degradation of the whole region. Prof. Powell exemplified the process by citing the Uinta Mountains as a broad platform similarly carved by an extensive erosion.

The following paper was read by LESTER F. WARD, entitled—

FIELD AND CLOSET NOTES ON THE FLORA OF WASHINGTON
AND VICINITY.

[Abstract.*]

Introductory Remarks.

This paper has resulted from a suggestion made to the writer in the spring of 1880, by a member of the Committee on Publications of this Society, relative to the need that exists for some special

---

* Mr. Ward's communication presented to the Society only a brief notice of the principal points of a monograph which he had prepared upon the flora of the District of Columbia. In view of the local character of his subject, and of the thorough and commendable manner in which it had been elaborated, the Committee on Communications recommended, and the General Committee authorized, the printing of a very full and copious abstract of the paper, which is given herewith.

treatise on the flora of this vicinity, and for a new and revised catalogue of the plants. While there now exists a provisional catalogue containing most of the species which have been collected or observed by botanists during the past six or seven years, it consists of so many small annual accretions, due to constant new discoveries, and contains withal so many blemishes and imperfections, incident to its hasty compilation and irregular growth, that it has ceased, in great part, to meet the demands of the present time. The elaboration of a systematic catalogue of the local flora was not, however, at the outset at all contemplated, but merely the presentation of certain notes and special observations on particular species, which had been made in the course of some nine years of pretty close attention to the vegetation, and somewhat varied and exhaustive field studies in this locality.

The flowering-time of most species here is much earlier than that given in the manuals, and is, moreover, in many cases, very peculiar and anomalous, rendering it important to collectors as well as interesting to botanists to have it definitely stated for a large proportion of the plants. It being thus necessary to extend the enumeration so far, it was thought that the remainder might as well be added, thus rendering it a complete catalogue of all the vascular plants known to occur here at the present time. To these has been appended the list of *musci* and *hepaticæ* prepared by the late Mr. Rudolph Oldberg for the *Flora Columbiana*, which has been left unchanged except in so far as was required to make it conform strictly to Sullivant's work which has long been the standard for this country. Dr. E. Foreman has also furnished the names of a few of the *Characeæ* collected by himself, and named by Prof. Farlow, of Cambridge, which, in the present unsettled state of the classification of the cryptogams, have, for convenience, been placed at the foot of the series.

In undertaking this compilation I have endeavored to resist the usual temptation of catalogue makers to expand their lists beyond the proportions which are strictly warranted by the concrete facts as revealed by specimens actually collected or species authentically observed ; but have been content to set down only such as I can either personally vouch for, or as are vouched for by others who have something more substantial than memory to rely upon ; preferring that a few species actually occuring but not yet seen should be omitted and afterwards supplied, rather than that others, sup-

5

posed to exist, but which cannot be found, should stand in the catalogue to be apologized for to those who would be glad to obtain
them. A few species, however, which are positively known to have
once occured within our limits, but which have been obliterated
within the recollection of persons now living, have been retained,
as well as several of which only a single specimen has been found ;
but in all such cases the facts are fully stated in the notes accompanying each plant.

Range of the Local Flora.

The extent of territory which has of late years been tacitly recognized by botanists here as constituting the area of what has been called
the *Flora Columbiana* is limited on the north by the Great Falls of
the Potomac, and on the south by the Mount Vernon estate in Virginia, and Marshall's just opposite this on the Maryland side of the
river, while it may reach back from the river as far as the divide
to the east, and as far westward as the foot of the Blue Ridge, so as
not to embrace any of the peculiarly mountain forms. Practically,
however, the east and west range is much more restricted and only
extends a few miles in either direction.

Comparison of the Flora of 1830 with that of 1880.

Washington and its vicinity has long been a field of botanical
research. The year 1825 witnessed the dissolution of the *Washington
Botanical Society*, which had for many years cultivated the science,
and the same year also saw the formation of the *Botanic Club*, which
continued the work, and in one respect, at least, excelled the former
in usefulness, since it has handed down to us of the present generation a valuable record in the form of a catalogue of the plants
then known to exist in this locality. This catalogue, which was
fittingly entitled *Floræ Columbianæ Prodromus*, and claimed to
exhibit " a list of all the plants which have as yet been collected,"
though now rare, and long out of print, is still to be found in a few
botanical libraries.

I have succeeded in securing a copy of this work, and have been
deeply interested in comparing the results then reached with those
which we are now able to present. A few of these comparisons are
well worth reproducing.

It should be premised that the *Prodromus* is arranged on the artificial system of Linnaeus, so that before the plants could be placed in juxtaposition they required to be re-arranged. This, however, was not the principal difficulty. Such extensive changes have taken place in the names of plants during the fifty years which have elapsed since that work appeared, (1830,) that it is only with the greatest difficulty that they can be identified. After much labor, I have succeeded in identifying the greater part of them, and in thus ascertaining about to what extent the two lists are in unison. This also reveals the extent to which each overlaps the other, and thus affords a sort of rude index to the changes which our flora has undergone in half a century. There are, however, as will be seen, many qualifying considerations which greatly influence these conclusions and diminish the value of the data compared.

The whole number of distinct names (species and varieties) enumerated in the *Prodromus* is 919. Of these 59 are mere synonyms or duplicate names for the same plant, leaving 860 distinct plants. I have succeeded in identifying 708 of these with certainty as among those now found, and six others, not yet clearly identified, should probably be placed in this class. This leaves 146 enumerated in the old catalogue which have not been found in recent investigations. [A classified list of these plants was presented and commented upon somewhat in detail.]

With regard to these 146 species, it must not be hastily concluded that they represent the disappearance from our flora of that number of plants. While they doubtless indicate such a movement to a certain extent, there are ample evidences that many of them can be accounted for in other ways. After careful consideration, I have been able to divide them into four principal classes arising out of—

1st. Errors on the part of those early botanists in assigning to them the wrong names.

2d. The introduction into the catalogue of adventitious and even of mere cultivated species, never belonging to the flora of the place.

3d. The undue extension by those collectors of the range of the local flora so as to make it embrace a portion of the maritime vegetation of the Lower Potomac or the Chesapeake Bay, and also the mountain flora of the Blue Ridge.

4th. The actual extermination and disappearance of indigenous plants during the fifty years that have intervened since they made their researches.

The assignment which I have made of each species to its appropriate class has been of course in great part conjectural and may be incorrect in many cases, while another botanist might have differed considerably in regard to special plants; yet it is not based on a general judgment drawn from my acquaintance with the present flora, but upon several kinds of special evidence, which in numerous instances has reversed my *prima facie* decision.

In the first place, I have carefully compared the range of each species as given in the text books to determine the probabilities for or against its being found here, and in the second place I have compared this list with the corresponding one of the species now found but not enumerated in the *Prodromus*. I have also endeavored to make due allowance on the one hand for the tendency above referred to to swell catalogues beyond their proper limits, and on the other for the well known fact that every flora is at all times undergoing changes.

It must not be forgotten, either, that half a century ago the surface of the entire country here must have presented a very different appearance from that which it presents now. The population of the District of Columbia in 1830, when it included a portion of Virginia, was only 39,834. It is now, exclusive of the Virginian part receded to that State, 177,638. To render the comparison more exact we may add to the latter number the present population of Alexandria county, amounting to 17,545, and we have in the place of 39,834 a population on substantially the same area of 195,183, or about five times as large. The population of Maryland in 1830 was 447,040; in 1880 it was 934,632, or considerably more than twice as large. That of Virginia in 1830 was 1,211,405. Virginia and West Virginia, embracing the same territory, now number 2,131,249 the population not having quite doubled: the retardation, however, as compared with Maryland, is doubtless due entirely to influences affecting the southern counties. There were doubtless large areas of primeval forest then within our limits which are now under cultivation, and a much greater variety of soil and woodland was then open to the researches of the botanist. As a consequence we ought to expect that it would sustain a much richer flora.

The general result at which I arrive by the process adopted may be summed up as follows:

1st. That 43 of these names, or 29 per cent. of them, belong to the first class and constitute errors in naming.

2d. That 12 of these plants, or 8 per cent., belong to the second class, or were simply cultivated species, and never belonged to this flora.

3d. That 10 of them, or 7 per cent., belong to the third class and were collected beyond the reasonable limits of our local flora.

4th. The remaining 81, or 56 per cent., belong to the fourth class, and represent *bona fide* discoveries in 1830 of species which either do not now occur or are so rare as to have escaped the investigations of the present generation of botanists.

With regard to the first of these classes, the large number of errors in naming cannot be considered any derogation from the ability or fidelity of the compilers of the *Prodromus* or their immediate predecessors, when we remember the very unsettled state that American botany was in at that time. Both names and authorities were badly confused, and errors were committed even by the most experienced botanists. For example, their *Corydalis glauca* as probably also their *C. aurea*, meant *C. flavula* which is now abundant, but omitted by them. Their *Arabis stricta* might have been *A. hirsuta* or *A. patens*, which are both now rare, though it was more probably a form of *A. laevigata*, as they seemed to be specially fond of drawing nice distinctions and expressing them by synonyms. Varieties, however, were scarcely recognized by them, the trinomial theory being then in its infancy. I might thus proceed to discuss all their supposed errors, but this is not necessary.

The second and third classes, amounting together to 16 per cent. of the alleged excess over the present flora, consist also of errors, but errors which it is much less easy to palliate. It is natural to wish to make as large a showing as possible, and the temptation to insert into a catalogue everything which by any construction can be claimed to belong there is rarely resisted. To show that this propensity still exists, it may be remarked that of the 1054 species enumerated in the preliminary catalogue of plants of this vicinity, published by the Potomac Side Naturalist's Club in 1876, 89, or about 8½ per cent. are now admitted by all not to have been seen here at that time, and have never been found by any one since, although nearly three hundred other species have since been added to the flora. This is certainly not a scientific method to proceed upon, and as already remarked, the present effort aims to eliminate to a great extent this source of error.

The 81 species constituting the fourth class remain, therefore, the

only ones to which any special interest attaches and for the determination of which the present somewhat laborious analysis of this
ancient document has been undertaken. For these, the botanists of
our times should make diligent search and perchance a few of them
may still be found. Assuming that they no longer exist, they do
not represent the whole number of plants that have disappeared
from our flora during the interval of fifty years. This could be
only on the assumption that the *Prodromus* was a complete record
of the flora at the time. This it certainly is not. The aggregate
number, exclusive of synonyms or duplicated names, which it contained was, as we saw, 860, which includes one cellular plant, viz:
Achara. We now identify, counting as was then done, species and
varieties, 1249 distinct vascular plants. While no doubt many of
these have been freshly appearing while others have been disappear-
ing, still, from the considerations above set forth, it is highly probable that the indigenous flora of 1830 was considerably larger than
that of 1880, and may have reached 1400 or 1500 vascular plants.
It would appear, therefore, that only a little over half the plants
actually existing were discovered by the botanists of that day, and
enumerated in their catalogue. If the proportion of disappearances
could be assumed to be the same for species not discovered as for
those discovered by them, this would raise the aggregate number to
considerably above one hundred, and perhaps to one hundred and
twenty-five.

The great number of present known species not enumerated in
the *Prodromus*, some of them among our commonest plants and a-
mounting in the aggregate to 535 species, is another point of interest,
since, after due allowance has been made for mistakes in naming
them, it remains clear on the one hand that these researches must
have been, compared with recent ones, very superficial; and on the
other, that, not to speak of fresh introductions, many plants now
common must have then been very rare, otherwise they would have
proved too obtrusive to be thus overlooked.

Localities of Special Interest to the Botanist.

The flora of a wild region is always more uniform than that of
one long subjected to human influences. The diversity in the former
is a natural consequence of the corresponding diversity in the surface and other physical features. In the latter it is due to condi-

tions arbitrarily imposed by man. A primeval flora is usually more rich in indigenous species, but the artificial changes caused by cultivation often offset this to a great extent by the introduction of foreign ones. This, however, greatly reduces its botanical interest.

In many respects the botanist looks at the world from a point of view precisely the reverse of that of other people. Rich fields of corn are to him waste lands; cities are his abhorrence, and great areas under high cultivation he calls "poor country;" while on the other hand the impenetrable forest delights his gaze, the rocky cliff charms him, thin-soiled barrens, boggy fens, and unreclaimable swamps and morasses are for him the finest lands in a State. He takes no delight in the "march of civilization;" the ax and the plow are to him symbols of barbarism, and the reclaiming of waste lands and opening up of his favorite haunts to cultivation he instinctively denounces as acts of vandalism. In him more than in any other class of mankind the poet's injunction—

" Woodman, spare that tree,"

touches a responsive cord. While all this may seem as absurd to some as does the withholding from tillage of great pleasure grounds in the form of hunting parks for the landed sporting gentry of Northern and Western Europe, still, when these parts of the world are compared with the artificially made deserts of Southeastern Europe and Western Asia, caused by the absence of such sentiments, there may, perhaps, be dimly recognized a "soul of good in things evil," if not a soul of wisdom in things ridiculous.

After the protracted subjection of a country to the conditions of civilization it gradually comes about that while the greater part of the surface falls under cultivation, more or less thorough, and the botanist is ultimately excluded from it, there will remain a few favored spots, which, from one cause or another, will escape and continue to form his favorite haunts. In the vicinity of large rivers, giving greater variety to the surface, or of rugged hills or mountains, this will be especially the case. As a country grows old large estates in the vicinity of cities fall into the possession of heirs who are engaged in mercantile or professional business, and neglect them, or they come into litigation lasting for years, and are thus happily abandoned to nature. These and other causes have operated in an especial manner in the surroundings of Washington, and there thus exist a large number of these green oases, as it were, interspersed over the otherwise botanical desert.

In consequence of this fact it requires experience in order to improve the facilities which the place affords. A botanist unacquainted with the proper localities for successful collection might spend a month almost in vain, and depart with the conviction that there was nothing here to be found. It may not be wholly peculiar, but these favored localities are here often of very limited extent, and in situations which from a distance afford no attraction to the collector. Civilization is, however, very perceptibly encroaching upon many of them, and it is feared that in another half century little will be left but a few bare rocks or inaccessible marshes.

In naming localities the principal authorities relied upon are: 1. A recent *Atlas of fifteen miles around Washington, including the County of Montgomery, Md., Compiled, Drawn, and Published from Actual Surveys, by G.˙M. Hopkins, C. E :* Philadelphia, 1879 ; and, 2, a military map of Northeastern Virginia, published in the work of General J. G. Barnard, on the *Defences of Washington*, 1821.

From the former the names of many roads, streams, estates, &c., have been obtained, while from the latter those of forts, batteries, &c., are often employed as more convenient. In this respect, however, much remains to be desired. While the military map is antiquated, the other is frequently defective in omitting what is required and incorrect in erroneously locating streams and other objects well known to the writer. In his extensive rambles he has learned many local names not found on the map, and in a few cases of special botanical interest, where names are wholly wanting, he has long been in the habit of designating the localities by names of his own christening, and for which he offers no apology.

The following are a few of the principal places of botanical interest which will be found to recur most frequently in the notes, and for this reason brief descriptions of them are appended.

1. *The Rock Creek Region.*—Rock Creek which forms the boundary line between Washington and Georgetown (West Washington), has escaped to a remarkable degree the inroads of agriculture and population. For the greater part of its length within the District of Columbia its banks are still finely wooded for some distance back, and afford a rich and varied field for botanical exploration. The character of the surface along Rock Creek is most beautiful and picturesque, often rocky and hilly with frequent deep ravines

coming down into the usually narrow bottom through which the creek flows. The stream itself is full of the most charming curves and the whole region is an ideal park. No one can see it without thinking how admirably it is adapted for a National Park. Such a park might be made to extend from Oak Hill Cemetery to the Military Road opposite Brightwood, having a width of a mile or a mile and a half. Not only every botanist but every lover of Art and Nature must sigh at the prospect, now not far distant, of beholding this region devastated by the ax and the plow. The citizens of Washington should speedily unite and strenuously urge upon Congress the importance of early rescuing this ready-made National Park from such an unfortunate fate.*

The Rock Creek Region is divided, so far as the designation of localities is concerned, into six sections. The first embracing the series of groves from Georgetown to Woodley Park on the right bank of the creek, is called Woodley. This section embraces several interesting ravines and in it are found many plants rare elsewhere, such as *Chamæ lirium, Carolinianum, Cypripedium pubescens, Hesperis matronalis* and *Liparis Lœselii*. In it is also a grove of the Hercules club (*Aralia spinosa.*) On the left bank of the creek lie the Kalorama Heights and some open woodland.

The *Woodley Park* section extends to the ravine which comes down opposite the old brick mill-ruin known as the Adams Mill. The timber here has been thinned out recently by the proprietors but not cleared off, and the vegetation has undergone a marked change. Several interesting plants have been found in Woodley Park, including the rare *Obolaria Virginica,* and the beautiful *Spiraea aruncus*. Above this the timber is heaviest on the left bank and some very fine ravines occur, at the head of one of which is a magnolia and sphagnum swamp where *Veratrum viride* and *Symplocarpus fœtidus* keep company with *Gonolibus obliquus* and *Pyrus*

---

* It is remarkable that when committees of Congress have been appointed, as has several times been done, to consider a site for a National Park, they have usually looked in other directions and have seemed to ignore the existence of this region, which is certainly the only one that possesses any natural claims. A mere carriage ride through such parts as are traversed by roads is wholly insufficient to afford an adequate idea of its merits from this point of view. For the greater part of the distance mentioned above this region is accessible only to footmen.

arbutifolia. Here, too, though well up towards the ford, has been found *Polemonium reptans,* not seen elsewhere.

This third section terminates at Piney Branch, and from here to Pierce's mill, and as far above as the mouth of Brood Branch, the fourth section extends. This section is well wooded on both sides and includes the enchanting Cascade run which leaps down over the most romantic rocks. Near Pierce's mill are many trees and shrubs, planted there years before, but now well naturalized. Among these are *Aralia spinosa, Xanthoxylum Americanum, Acer saccharinum, Pinus strobus,* and *Carya alba.* Below the mill on the creek bottom is a long-abandoned nursery of *Populus alba* and *Acer dasycarpum,* from which many of the trees of the city may have been supplied.

From Broad branch to the Military road is the fifth and perhaps most interesting section of the Rock Creek Region. On the left bank lie the once noted Crystal Springs, and though the buildings are removed, the springs remain unchanged. Here have been found *Ophioglossum vulgatum, Anychia dichotoma,* and *Perilla ocimoides,* as well as *Tipularia discolor.* On the right bank and above Blagden's mill is a bold bluff in a short bend of the creek forming a sort of promontory upon which there grows *Gaultheria procumbens,* the winter-green or checkerberry, this being its only known locality within our limits. Half a mile farther up and back upon the wooded slope is the spot on which stand a dozen or more fine trees of the Table Mountain Pine, (*P. pungens.*) Here also was first found *Pycnanthenum Torreyi.*

To these there must be added a sixth section extending from the Brightwood road to the north corner of the District of Columbia which lies near Rock Creek. For the first mile there is little of interest, the cultivated land approaching the creek and the low hills near its banks being covered with a short second growth of scrub pine and black-jack. But above the Claggett estate on the right bank, and to some extent on both sides, lies the largest forest within our limits. This wood belongs, I learn, to the Carroll estate and is so designated in this catalogue. In it have been found very many most interesting plants. It was the first extensive tract found for the crowfoot (*Lycopodium complanatum*) and still constitutes the most reliable and abundant source known of this plant. Its present fame, however, rests upon its hybrid oaks, of which some most interesting forms have been found there. [See Field and Forest,

October and November, 1875; Botanical Gazette, October, 1880, p. 123.]   Here also grows very sparingly *Microstylis ophioglossoides*, and quite abundantly *Pyrola elliptica* and *P. secunda*.   It is also a rich locality for many other species rare elsewhere.

2. *The Upper Potomac Region.*—The flora of the left bank of the Potomac is, in many respects, very unlike that of any other locality within our limits.   A mile above Georgetown, and commencing from the recently constructed outlet lock of the Chesapeake and Ohio canal, there exists a broad and low strip of country formerly known by the name of Carberry Meadows, lying between the canal and the river, and extending to the feeder of the canal, a distance of about three and a half miles.   This interval is relieved by two convenient landmarks, viz., one mile above the outlet lock, a grist-mill and guano factory, popularly known as Eads' mill; and a mile further, the celebrated Chain Bridge.   Little Falls, proper, begin a hundred yards above the bridge, and extend half a mile or more.   The region above the bridge will, therefore, be designated as Little Falls.   The flats terminate in a remarkable knoll or small hillock of very regular outline and abrupt sides, which, from the combined effects of the feeder on one side, and large overflows from it below, becomes practically an island, and is well known to all as High Island.   These river flats are, in most places, covered with large boulders of the characteristic gneiss rock of the country.   In some parts the surface is very rough, and numerous pools or small ponds of water occur.   Overflows and leakages from the canal cause large sloughs and quagmires, while annual ice-gorges crush down the aspiring fruticose vegetation.   All these circumstances lend variety to the locality, and, as might be expected, the flora partakes largely of this characteristic.   It would prolong this sketch unduly to enumerate all the rare and interesting plants which this region has contributed to our vegetable treasures, but conspicuous among them are *Polygonum amphibium*, var. *terrestre, Isanthus cœruleus, Herpestis nigrescens, Brasenia peltata, Cyperus virens,* and *Nesœa verticillata,* all of which recur below Ead's mill ; *Ammannia humilis,* a remarkable variety of *Salix nigra,* (*S. nigra* var. *Wardi, Bebb.*) *Salix cordata,* and *S. longifolia;* as also *Spiranthes latifolia,* and *Samolus valerandi* var. *Americanus, Vitis vulpina* and *Panicum pauciflorum,* which may be found between this point and the bridge, while at the Little Falls we are favored with *Paronychia dichotoma, Œnothera fruticosa,* var. *lineare*

(very distinct from the type) and *Cconothus ovatus* : also *Ranunculus pusillus* and *Utricularia gibba*. But rich and varied as are these lower flats, they are excelled by High Island, the flora of which is by far the most exuberant of all within the knowledge of botanists. Here we find *Jeffersonia diphylla, Caulophyllum thalictroides, Erigenia bulbosa, Silene nivea, Valeriana pauciflora, Erythronium albidum, Iris cristata*, and a great number of others of our most highly prized plants, many of which are found nowhere else.

Above the feeder is a series of islands in the river lying for the most part near the Maryland shore, and to which the maps, so far as I can learn, assign no names. The first of these lies well out in the river and has been made to form a part of the feeder-dam. It is low and frequently overflowed, and has not, as yet, furnished many rare plants, though here *Arabis dentata* and some others have been found. It has been designated *Feeder-dam Island*. The second is half or three-quarters of a mile above, lies higher, and is covered with a very dense and luxuriant herbaceous vegetation and fine trees, chiefly of Box Elder, *Negundo aceroides*, from which circumstance and the peculiar impression which the long gracefully pendent staminate flower of these trees produced on the occasion of its first discovery by a botanical party it received the name of *Box Elder Island*. The third island is a short distance above the last, has a more elevated central portion and a similar vegetation. Here was found, on our first visit, and also on subsequent ones, *Delphinium tricorne*, and for this contribution to the Flora Columbiana it was christened *Larkspur Island*. The fourth of these islands is, in many respects, similar to the two last described, and upon it stands the only indigenous specimen of *Acer saccharinum* yet found here. It has, therefore, been appropriately named *Sugar-maple Island*. *Erythronium albidum, Trillium sessile, Jeffersonia diphylla* and similar species abound on all these islands, while on the Larkspur Island, besides the *Delphinium*, has also been found *Phacelia Purshii*. The beauty of these natural flower-gardens in the months of April and May is unequaled in my experience. The light and rich alluvial soil causes the vegetation to shoot up with magic rapidity at the first genial rays of the vernal sun, and often the harbinger of spring, *Erigenia bulbosa*, true to its name, will greet the delighted rambler in late February or early March.

The opposite, or Virginia side of the Upper Potomac, consists entirely of bold bluffs, interrupted by deep ravines, often containing wild torrents and dashing cascades. Here the flora, though less rich and varied, is also characteristic and interesting, and embraces, among other rare things, *Rhododendron maximum, Iris crestata, Scutellaria saxatilis, Pycnanthemum Torreyi, Solidago rupestris* and *S. virga-aurea,* var. *humilis.* On the Maryland side and a mile above the uppermost point thus far mentioned, is the Cabin John run, which the botanist celebrates more for its walking fern (*Camptosorus rhizophyllus*) than for the world-renowned arch that spans it.

The next most prolific source of interesting plants is the region of the Great Falls. The collecting grounds begin a mile or more below at Broad Water. On both sides of the canal the country is excellent, rocky and wooded, with stagnant pools and sandy hillocks. On these rocks grow *Sedum telephoides* and near Sandy Landing are found *Vitis vulpina, Arabis patens, A. hirsuta* and *Triosteum angustifolium.* In the pools have been found *Carex decomposita, Potamogeton hybridus* and *P. pauciflorus,* while on a rocky headland a large "water-pocket" has yielded my only specimen of the white water lily (*Nymphæa odorata*). *Cratægus parvifolia, Rumex verticillatus Steironema lanceolatum,* and last but not least, *Nasturium lacustre,* have also rewarded my researches in this singular and rather weird region.

On the opposite side of the river the site of the ancient canal around the Falls has proved very fertile in botanical trophies. *Polygala ambigua* is found near the boat landing, while by climbing the cliffs below this point the native of more northern climes may gaze once more upon his familiar Hemlock Spruce, *Tsuga Canadensis.* Difficult Run, a mile farther down, though indeed difficult of approach, repays the effort with *Podostemon ceratophyllus, Smilacina stellata, Potamogeton Claytonii,* and numerous other herbal treasures.

3. *The Lower Potomac Region.*

Passing next to the lower Potomac, the localities of special interest are, 1. Custis Spring, opposite the Arlington estate, with the extensive marsh below, where *Sagittaria pusilla, Discopleura capillacea, Cyperus erythrorhizus,* and other rare species are alone known to grow. 2. The point and bay below Jackson City, known as Roach's run, where are found, among others, *Scrophularia nodosa,*

Tripsacum dactyloides and *Pycnanthemum lanceolatum*. 3. Four Mile run, half way to Alexandria, not yet sufficiently explored, including the vicinity of Fort Scott to the northwest, where *Clematis ochroleuca* and *Asclepias quadrifolia* may be collected ; and, 4. Hunting creek, a large estuary below Alexandria, including Cameron run, the stream which debouches into it, with its tributaries, Back Lick run and Holmes' run, which unite to form it. Here have been found, at various points, *Clematis ochroleuca, Gonolobus hirsutus, Itea Virginica, Geranium columbinum, Micranthemum Nuttallii, Habenaria virescens, Quercus macrocarpa, Carex gracillima, Geum strictum, Galium asprellum,* and very many other rare plants.

On the left bank of the lower Potomac the chief locality of interest is a large wooded area below the Government Hospital for the Insane. This has proved a rich hunting ground for the botanist, and has yielded *Carex pallescens, Carex Woodii, Gonolobus hirsutus, Silene armeria, Parietaria Pennsylvanica, Myosotis arvensis, Scutellaria nervosa,* &c., &c. *Asplenium angustifolium* is known only at Marshall Hall, where it has been reported by Mr. O. M. Bryan, while opposite Fort Foote Mr. Zumbrock has found *Myriophyllum spicatum,* and opposite Alexandria Professor Comstock and Miss Willets have discovered *Plantago cordata.*

4. *The Terra Cotta Region.*

This embraces some low grounds and undulating barrens near the terra cotta works, at Terra Cotta Station, on the Metropolitan Branch of the Baltimore and Ohio railroad, three miles from the city, and also a small swamp a quarter of a mile beyond, and to the eastward. Here on the dry ground have been found *Onosmodium Virginianum, Lespedeza Stuvei, Clitoria Mariana,* and *Habenaria lacera ;* and in the swamp *Aster æstivus, Solida stricta, Woodwardia Virginica, Asclepias rubra, Poterium Canadense,* and numerous other plants rare or absent in other localities.

5. *The Reform School Region.*

This locality is very limited in extent, but has proved one of the most fertile in botanical rarities. Its nucleus consists of a little swampy spot a short distance to the south of the National Reform School, in which is located a beautiful spring ; but the woody tract of country surrounding this and stretching southward and eastward some distance has also proved very fruitful. In the different portions of this region have been discovered *Phlox maculata, Melanthium Virginicum, Bartonia tenella, Lespedeza Stuvei, Desmodium Marilandicum* and *D. cilare, Buchnera Americana, Fimbristylis capillaris, Quercus prinoides, Carex bullata*, and *Gentiana ochroleuca*, most of which do not occur at all elsewhere.

6. *The Holmead Swamp Region.*

Like the last, this locality is quite circumscribed in area, but like it, too, it is rich in interesting plants. It occupies a ravine leading to Piney Branch from the east at the point where the continuation of Fourteenth street crosses that stream. The road connecting the last named with the Rock Creek Church road, and which is called Spring street, follows this valley. The collecting grounds are on the south side of this road and in the springy meadow along the rill. The timber has long been cut off, but the boggy character of the ground has thus far protected it from cultivation. The pasturing of animals on it during a portion of the year has latterly become a serious detriment to the growth of plants. Mr. Hoimead, who owns it and lives near by, has kindly permitted botanists to investigate it for their purposes. Here have been found *Ludwigia hirsuta, Drosera rotundifolia Asclepias rubra, Xyris flexuosa, Fuirena squarrosa, Rhinchospora alba, Coreopsis discoidea* and the beautiful *Calopogon pulchellus* the most showy of our orchids.

In addition to these specially fertile tracts there are many other localities of great interest where valuable accessions to our flora have been made, and which will be particularly designated under the names of these species. It will suffice here to mention a wet meadow between the National Driving Park and Bladensburg, where, in a very diminutive spot, *Sarracenia purpurea, Viola lanceolata*, and *Carex bullata*, the two first wholly unknown elsewhere, have been discovered; a marsh a mile from Bladensburg, near the millrace, where only the majestic *Stenanthium robustum* has been seen; a little swamp near the Sligo creek, between the Riggs and Blair roads, where the Hartford fern (*Lygodium palmatum*) grows sparingly; and another between Bladensburg and the Maryland Agricultural College, where *Solidago elliptica, Ascyrum stans*, and *Lycopodium complanatum*, var. *Sabinæfolium*, have been found. The

Eastern branch region is not specially rich in floral treasures, but on its banks and marshes some good things appear. *Habenaria virescens, Steironema laceolatum, Eleocharis quadrangulata, Scirpus fluviatilis, Ranunculus ambigens,* and *Salix Russelliana* are among these, though some of them are found elsewhere.

Flowering time of Plants.

It has already been remarked that most species flower at **Washington** much earlier than at points farther north or the dates given in the manuals. In consequence of this, a botanist unacquainted with this fact, and accustomed to those climates and to relying upon the books, would be likely to be behind the season throughout the year, and fail to get the greater part of the plants he desired. With all my efforts to make allowance for this fact, I have frequently been sorely disappointed and was at last driven to making a careful record, preserving and correcting it from year to year, of the *flowering time* of plants in this locality. The notes on this subject appended to nearly every species enumerated in the list embody the general results of these observations and may in the main be relied upon. The expressions used are not loose conjectures, but are in the nature of compilations from recorded data. In most cases an allowance of two weeks may be made for the difference in seasons though rarely more and often less. Certain plants, as for example, *Tipularia discolor,* flower at almost exactly the same time every year. Occasionally, however, one will vary a month or more in a quite unaccountable way. But any one who has watched the periodical changes of the general vegetation for a series of years and recorded his observations, will more and more realize the exactness even of these complex biological phenomena which depend so absolutely upon uniform astronomical events.

From this point of view the season which presents the greatest variation and also, for this and other reasons, the greatest interest is the spring. There are a few plants which may sometimes be found in flower here in January, such as *Stellaria media, Taraxacum dens-leonis* or *Acer dasycarpum* (collected Jan. 17, 1876, in the city) in favored places, but these will bloom at any time when a few days of mild weather with sunshine can come to revive them. There are, however, several strictly vernal species which bloom quite regularly in the latter part of February, such as *Symplocarpus fœ-*

tidus, Chrysosplenium Americanum, and often *Anemone hepatica.* The number regularly found in flower in March is quite large and in special years very large. It was of course impossible to make observations every day of any year, but taking a number of years my observations cover nearly every day of the spring season. As showing the number of these early vernal species and also how widely the seasons may differ, the following facts are presented:

In the year 1878 seventeen species had actually been seen in flower and noted up to March 24th. I did not go out again that year until April 7, when I enumerated forty-six additional species, making sixty-three in all up to that date. This was an exceptionally early season. The next spring, that of 1879, was a backward one, as is shown by the fact that while I had visited the same localities, and taken notes with equal care only thirty-three species had been seen in flower up to April 13th: twenty-nine species which had been seen in flower on April 7th, 1878, were not yet in flower in the same localities on April 13th, 1879. There appeared to be about three week's difference in these two seasons. The last season, 1880, was again an early one, though less so than 1878. It was, however, near enough to the average to render the facts observed of great value. The following are a few of them: On February 29th, seven species were seen in flower in the Rock Creek region. On April 4th, thirty were enumerated on the Virginia side of the Potomac, above the Aqueduct Bridge. On April 11th, eleven were seen in addition to those previously enumerated in the Eastern Branch region: and on the 18th of April, High Island was visited, and twenty-nine added to all previously recorded, three of which were then in fruit. The total to this date was therefore seventy species. This season I concluded was a week or ten days later than that of 1878, and as much earlier than that of 1879.*

---

* Since the above was written the present season (1881) has passed its vernal period. It has proved still more backward than 1879 and the latest spring thus far observed. On April 3d, I made my first excursion and visited the Virginia side of the Potomac above Rosslyn. Only 7 species were seen in flower including *Alnus serrulata* which doubtless can be obtained much earlier in ordinary years, but has been overlooked. Besides *Draba verna,* a January species, and *Anemone hepatica,* a February one, the only herbaceous flower found was *Sanguinaria Canadensis.* On April 10th, High Island was visited, but only 8 species could be added to the above 7, and several of these, as *Jeffersonia diphylla, Dicentra cucullaria, Saxifraga Virginiensis, Erythronium Americanum,* and *Stellaria pu-*

We may now inquire what some of these early plants are.   The following have been observed in flower in February :

Chrysosplenium Americanum, February 17, 1878.
Anemone Hepatica, February 20, 1876.
Salix Babylonica, February 22, 1874.
Populus alba, February 22, 1874.
Draba verna, February 24, 1878.
Acer dasycarpum, February 24, 1878,
Stellaria media, February 29, 1880.
Cerastium viscosum, February 29, 1880.
Claytonia Virginica, February 29, 1880.
Acer rubrum, February 29, 1880.
Symplocarpus fœtidus, February 29, 1880.

To these should, perhaps, be added *Equisetum hyemale*, which was found February 17, 1878, near the receiving reservoir with the spikes well advanced, quite contrary to the books which make it fruit in summer.

In addition to the above, which may often also be seen later, the the following have been noted flowering in March:

Populus alba, March 3, 1874,
Viola pedata, March 5, 1876.
Houstonia cœrulea, March 5, 1876.
Obolaria Virginica, March 5, 1876.
Dentaria heterophylla, March 8, 1874.
Poa brevifolia, March 8, 1874.
Capsella Bursa-pastoris, March 10, 1878.
Lamium amplexicaule, March 10, 1878.
Lindera Benzoin, March 10, 1878.
Epigaea repens, March 15, 1874.
Ulmus fulva, March 15, 1874.
Luzula campestris, March 15, 1874.
Saxifraga Virginiensis, March 16, 1879.
Sanguinaria Canadensis, March 17, 1878.
Sisymbrium Thaliana, March 17, 1878.

---

bera, were very sparingly out. Cold weather continued to the end of the third week in April, and on April 24th, when High Island was again visited and a thorough canvas made, only 22 additional plants could be found there, and the whole number seen to that date was 46. The conclusion was that up to that time the season was about three weeks later than that of 1880.

Salix tristis, March 17, 1877.
Populus grandidentata, March 21, 1880.
Corydalis flavula, March 22, 1874.
Thalictrum anemonoides, March 24, 1878.
Dentaria laciniata, March 24, 1878.
Antennaria plantaginifolia, March 24, 1878.
Erodium cicutarium, March 27, 1874.
Erigenia bulbosa, March 28, 1875.
Cardamine hirsuta, March 30, 1879.

It is about the first of April, especially in early years, that the vegetation seems to receive the greatest impetus. This is well shown by the following list of species seen in flower during the first week in April:

Ulmus Americana, April 1, 1873.
Jeffersonia diphylla, April 2, 1876.
Cardamine rhomboidea, April 2, 1876.
Stellaria pubera, April 2, 1876.
Thaspium aureum, April 2, 1876.
Euphorbia commutata, April 2, 1876.
Alnus serrulata, April 3, 1881.
Ranunculus abortivus, April 4, 1880.
Dicentra Cucullaria, April 4, 1880.
Arabis laevigata, April 4, 1880.
Viola tricolor. var. arvensis, April 4, 1880.
Vicia Caroliniana, April 4, 1880.
Amelanchier Canadensis, April 4, 1880.
Nepeta Glechoma, April 4, 1880.
Sassafras officinale, April 4, 1880.
Carpinus Americana, April 4, 1880.
Ostrya Virginica, April 4, 1880.
Erythroneum Americanum, April 4, 1880.
Barbarea vulgaris, April 5, 1874.
Pedicularis Canadensis, April 5, 1874.
Mertensia Virginica, April 5, 1874.
Ranunculus abortivus, var. micranthus, April 7, 1878.
Ranunculus repens, April 7, 1878.
Asimina triloba, April 7, 1878.
Caulophyllum thalictroides, April 7, 1878.
Arabis dentata, April 7, 1878.

Barbarea praecox, April 7, 1874.
Sisymbrium Alliaria, April 7, 1878.
Viola cucullata, April 7, 1878.
Viola striata, April 7, 1878.
Viola glabella, April 7, 1878.
Iouidium concolor, April 7, 1878.
Silene, Pennsylvanica, April 7, 1878.
Cerastium vulgatum, April 7, 1878.
Cerastium oblongifolium, April 7, 1878.
Geranium, maculatum, April 7, 1878.
Oxalis corniculata, April 7, 1878.
Cercis Canadensis, April 7, 1878.
Potentilla Canadensis, April 7, 1878.
Thaspium trifoliatum, April 7, 1878.
Cornus florida, April 7, 1878.
Chrysogonum, Virginianum, April 7, 1878.
Senecio aureus, April 7, 1878.
Fraxinus viridis, April 7, 1878.
Phlox divaricata, April 7, 1878.
Lithospermum arvense, April 7, 1878.
Betula nigra, April 7, 1878.
Populus monilifera, April 7, 1878.
Arisaema triphyllum, April 7, 1878.
Erythronium albidum, April 7, 1878.
Trillium sessile, April 7, 1878.

My special observations on the vernal flowering time of plants
extend about two weeks later or to the end of the third week in
April, after which the great number of plants in bloom, including
the amentaceous trees, render it difficult to pursue the investigation,
while at the same time the facts become less valuable. The results
for the second and third weeks of April, always excluding all previously enumerated, are as follows :

Arabis lyrata, April 9, 1876.
Fraxinus pubescens, April 11, 1880.
Salix cordata, April 11, 1880.
Salix purpurea, April 11, 1880.
Vaccinium corymbosum, April 12, 1880.
Carex platyphylla, April 12, 1880.
Poa annua, April 12, 1874.

Thalictrum dioicum, April 14, 1876.

Rhus aromatica, April 14, 1878.

Phlox subulata, April 14, 1878.

Arabis patens, April 18, 1880.

Cardamine hirsuta, var sylvatica, April 18, 1880.

Negundo aceroides, April 18, 1880.

Erigeron bellidifolius, April 18, 1880.

Krigia Virginica, April 18, 1880.

Sisyrinchium Bermudiana, April 18, 1880.

Carex laxiflora, April 18, 1880.

Carex Emmonsii, April 18, 1880.

Melica mutica, April 18, 1880.

Anemone nemorosa, April 19, 1874.

Viola cucullata, var. cordata, April 19, 1874.

Dirca palustris, April 19, 1874.

Carex Pennsylvanica, April 19, 1874.

Lathyrus venosus, April 21, 1878.

Ribes rotundifolia, April 21, 1878.

Salix nigra, var. Wardi, April 21, 1878.

We thus see that a single collector has in the course of eight year's operations actually observed and noted eleven species in bloom in February, 24 more in March, 51 additional in the first week of April, and 26 others during the second and third weeks of April or 112 up to April 21.

It should be remarked that there is no doubt that if the same localities in which the large numbers were observed on April 2 1876, April 4, 1880, and April 7, 1878 had been visited in the last days of March of those years quite a number of these plants would have been found sufficiently advanced to demand a place in the lists, and thus the month of March would have been credited with so many here set down for the first week in April. Probably, all things considered, not less than fifty species in certain favored seasons either reach or pass by their flowering-time by the end of March.

In arranging the above lists the order of dates has of course taken precedence, but where several are enumerated under one date the natural order is followed.

It is scarcely necessary to suggest a caution to collectors against relying upon these dates in making collections. They represent the earliest observations and not the average. In most cases an allowance of at least one week should be made for the full blooming of all the individuals of any given species. In all cases, however, one or more individuals were actually seen in flower and sufficiently advanced for collection, otherwise no note was taken. The *Carices* of course had not advanced to developed perigynia, and many plants whose inflorescence is centrifugal or centripetal, or which develop fruit while retaining their flowers, should be looked for at a later stage.

Autumnal Flowering.

One of the most interesting peculiarities of the flora of this vicinity is that of the second-blooming of vernal species, which in most cases takes place quite late in the fall. [See *Field and Forest*, April–June, 1878, Vol. III, p. 172.] In addition to the seven species observed and published in 1878, I have noted more than as many others manifesting this habit, and it is probable that still others will yet be added. The following is a list of those thus far recorded with the dates at which they were observed and which may be compared with those of their regular vernal period :

Ranunculus abortivus, var. micranthus, November 28, 1875.
Cardamine hirsuta, October 3, 1880.
Viola pedata, var. bicolor, September 22, and December 8, 1878
Viola striata, September 10, 1876.
Fragaria Virginiana, September 22, 1878.
Rubus villosus, September 22, and October 27, 1878.
Lonicera Japonica, October 13, 1878.
Houstonia purpurea, October 13, 1878.
Houstonia purpurea, var. angustifolia, September 12, 1880.
Houstonia cærulea, September 7, 1879.
Vaccinium stamineum, October 13, 1878.
Rhododendron nudiflorum, October 13, 1878.
Sabbatia angularis, October 27, 1878.
Phlox divaricata, October 16, 1873.
Echium vulgare, October 8, 1880.
Veronica officinalis, October 8, 1873.
Agrostis scabra, November 12, 1876.

To this list of seventeen should perhaps be added *Stellaria pubera*, which instead of a vernal and autumnal period, has two vernal periods as described under that species in the systematic notes.

Salix longifolia has this year (1881,) flowered twice ; once in April and again in June.

Autumnal blooming, in so far as it is peculiar to this climate, may be chiefly attributed to the tolerably regular occurrence here of a hot and dry season in midsummer. This usually begins towards the end of June and ends about the middle of August. During this period, in some seasons, the ground and vegetation become parched and dried up, so that vegetal processes in many plants cease almost as completely as in the opposite season of cold. From this dormant state, the warm and often copious rains of the latter part of August revive them, as do the showers of spring, and they begin anew their regular course of changes. The frosts of October usually cut their career short before maturity is reached, but in some cases two crops of seed are produced. In addition to this, there frequently also occurs a very warm term in November, often extending far into December, and of this certain species take advantage and push forth their buds and flowers.

Albinos.

Well defined albinos have been collected of the following species

Desmodium nudiflorum.
Liatris graminifolia.
Rhododendron nudiflorum.
Vinca minor.
Mertensia Virginica.
Sabbatia angularis.
Pontederia cordata.

The green flowered variety of *Trillium sessile* is also common, and *Gonolobus obliquus* exhibits on High Island this same anomalous feature. *Carex tentaculata* having the spikes perfectly white, as if etiolated, was found June 14 of this year, (1881,) on the Eastern Branch marsh. This last phenomenon was certainly due neither to maturity or disease, but was a mere *lusus naturæ*.

Double Flowers, &c.

Thalictrum anemonoides, Ranunculus bullosus, Claytonia Virginica, and *Rubrus Canadensis*, have been found with the flowers much doubled as in cultivation.

Hydrangea arborescens occasionally has the outer circle of petals expanded as in cultivation.

Rudbeckia fulgida has been found with all its rays tubular but of the usual length.

Statistical View of the Flora.

In order to present a clear view of the general character of the vegetation of the District of Columbia and the adjacent country, I have made a somewhat careful analysis of the large groups and families, and comparison of them not only with each other, but with the same groups and families in larger areas and other local floras. The general results are presented below.

It is important to remark that in all enumerations, it is not simply the number of *species*, as at present recognized, but the number of *diffrent plants*, (species and varieties,) that is employed. The reason for doing this is that in very many cases, well marked varieties are eventually made species, and if two plants really differ there is little probability that they will ever be merged into one species without that difference being indicated by some difference of name. The aim has therefore been to take account of the number of plants without regard to the manner in which they are named.

The whole number of vascular plants now known to this flora, as catalogued in the list appended to this paper, is 1249, and these belong to 527 different genera, or about 2⅓ species to each genus. These are distributed among the several systematic series, classes, and divisions, as follows:

Groups.	Genera.	Species and varieties.
Polyptelæ	174	356
Gamopetalæ	169	389
Total Dichlamydeæ	343	745
Monochlamydeæ (Apetalæ)	47	124
Total Dicotyledons	390	869
Monocotyledons	112	331
Gymnospermæ (Coniferæ)	4	7
Total Phænogamia	506	1,207
Cryptogamia	21	42
Total vascular plants	527	1,249

The percentages of the total are as follows:

Polypetalæ	33	29
Gamopetalæ	32	31
Total Dichlamydeæ	65	60
Monochlamydeæ (Apetalæ)	9	10
Total Dicotyledons	74	70
Monocotyledons	21	26
Gymnospermæ (Coniferæ)	1	1
Total Phænogamia	96	97
Cryptogamia	4	3

Large Orders.

The sixteen largest orders arranged according to the number of species, are as follows:

	Genera.	Species and varieties.
1. Compositæ	53	149
2. Gramineæ	43	110
3. Cyperaceæ	10	108
4. Leguminosæ	24	57
5. Rosaceæ	15	46
6. Labiatæ	23	42
7. Cruciferæ	16	33
8. Scrophulariaceæ	15	32
9. Filices	16	30
10. Ranunculaceæ	7	27
11. Ericaceæ	11	26
12. Cupuliferæ	7	26
13. Orchidaceæ	12	24
14. Liliaceæ	18	24
15. Polygonaceæ	3	23
16. Umbelliferæ	17	22

The whole number of systematic orders represented in our District is 116, of which sixteen, or 14 per cent. furnish 55 per cent. of the genera and 62 per cent. of the species.

Large Genera.

The fifteen large genera arranged according to the number of plants are the following :

Species and varieties.

1. Carex _____ 70
2. Aster _____ 21
3. Panicum _____ 19
4. Solidago_____ 18
5. Quercus _____ 18
6. Polygonum _____ 16
7. Desmodium_____ 14
8. Salix_____ 14
9. Juncus _____ 14
10. Viola _____ 13
11. Cyperus _____ 12
12. Ranunculus _____ 11
13. Eupatorium _____ 11
14. Helianthus_____ 10
15. Asclepias _____ 10

Thus fifteen, or less than three per cent., of the genera furnish 271, or nearly 22 per cent. of the species.

Introduced Species.

The whole number of introduced plants enumerated in the sub-joined catalogue is 193, of which 15 are supposed or known to be indigenous to other parts of the United States.* These are distributed through the several larger groups as follows:

---

* These are the following :

Xanthoxylum Americanum.   Symphoricarpus racemosus.
Trifolium repens.   Symphoricarpus vulgaris.
Prunus Chicasa.   Catalpa bignonioides.
Rosa setigera.   Maclura aurantiaca.
Philadelphus inodorus.   Populus grandidentata.
Ribes rotundifolium.   Poa annua.
Ribes rubrum.   Pinus Strobus.
Passiflora incarnata.

	Old World.	United States.	Total.
Polypetalous	65	8	73
Gamopetalous	54	3	57
Apetalous	28	2	30
Monocotyledonous	31	1	32
Coniferæ	--	1	1
Total	178	15	193

It will be seen that the introduced plants amount to 15.5 per cent, of the total flora.

The several orders to which these belong, are shown in the summary.

Shrubby Species.

Of the 342 "Forest Trees" enumerated in Sargent's preliminary catalogue of 1880, this flora embraces 85, or 24.8 per cent., of which 65 are large enough to have the dignity of timber trees. Of these 85, 25 are in the Polypetalous Division, but only 12 of this latter number are large; 9 are in the Monopetalous Division, all but 2 of which are large; 44 are in the Apetalous Division, 39 of which are large; and the remaining 7 are Coniferous, all full-sized trees.

The whole number of species which are shrubby or woody above ground is 194, which is 15.5 per cent. of the whole; they are distributed as follows:

Polypetalous	83
Gamopetalous	36
Apetalous (Monochlamydeous)	64
Monocotyledonous (Endogenous)	4
Gymnospermous (Coniferous)	7
Total	194

For further particulars the reader can consult the Summary at the end of the catalogue.

Comparisons with other Floras.

While these facts are of great interest in affording a clear conception of the character of our flora, they do not aid us in determining in what respects it is peculiar or marks a departure from

those of other portions of the country, or from that of the country
at large. To institute comparisons with other local floras would of
course carry me much too far for the general purpose of this paper,
but it is both more interesting and more practicable to confront a
few of the above results with similar ones, drawn from a consideration of a large part of the United States. For this purpose, as not
only most convenient but as least liable to embrace facts calculated
to vitiate the comparisons, I have chosen that portion of the United
States situated east of the Mississippi river, and for the most part
well covered by *Gray's Manual of Botany* for the Northern portion
and *Chapman's Flora of the Southern States* for the Southern. The
plants described in these works are conveniently collected into one
series by the second edition of *Mann's Catalogue*, published under
the supervision of the authorities at Cambridge, in 1872. Many
changes have since been made in the names, &c., and a few new
species added, but these are not sufficient to affect the general conclusions to be drawn from the following comparative tables.

Comparison of Species and Varieties.

The number of species and varieties of vascular plants enumerated in the work above referred to is 4,034, of which the 1,249 of
the flora of Washington, by groups, is as follows:

	Species and varieties in the		Per Cent.
	Eastern U. S.	Flora Columbiana.	
Polypetalæ	1,115	356	32
Gamopetalæ	1,314	389	30
Total Dichlamydeæ	2,429	745	31
Monochlamydeæ (Apetalæ)	349	124	36
Total Dicotyledons	2,778	869	31
Monocotyledons (Endogens)	1,034	331	32
Gymnospermæ	28	7	25
Total Phænogamia	3,840	1,207	31
Cryptogamia	194	42	22
Total vascular plants	4,034	1,249	31

Comparison of Genera.

The whole number of genera in the flora of the Eastern United States is 1065. That of the Flora Columbiana, as already stated is 527. This is over 49 per cent., a much larger proportion than was shown by a comparison of the species. A comparison of the genera by classes, gives the following results:

| | Genera represented in the | | Per Cent. |
	Eastern U. S.	Flora Columbiana.	
Polypetalæ _____	340	174	51
Gamopetalæ _____	379	169	45
Total Dichlamydeæ _____	719	343	48
Monochlamydeæ (Apetalæ)_____	97	47	48
Total Dicotyledons_____	816	390	48
Monocotyledons _____	198	112	57
Gymnospermæ _____	12	4	33
Total Phænogamia _____	1,026	506	49
Cryptogamia _____	39	21	54
Total vascular plants_____	1,065	527	49

The percentages here range from 33 in the Gymnosperms to 57 in the Monocotyledons, averaging between 49 and 50, whereas in the similar comparisons for species they ranged from 22 in the Cryptogams to 36 in the *Monochlamydeæ*. This result was to be expected since as the groups increase, the number represented in any local flora should be proportionally larger. For example, 116 orders out of the 156 are represented here, which is upwards of 74 per cent.

Comparison of Large Orders.

It will be interesting to compare in a manner similar to the foregoing, the number of species in several of the largest orders. For this purpose we may use the same orders mentioned a few pages back as the richest in species of any belonging to this flora. The comparison may then be shown as follows:

Orders.	Eastern U. S.	Flora Col.	Per Cent.
1. Compositæ	497	149	30
2. Gramineæ	297	110	37
3. Cyperaceæ	357	108	30
4. Leguminosæ	208	57	27
5. Rosaceæ	104	46	44
6. Labiatæ	121	42	35
7. Cruciferæ	76	33	43
8. Scrophulariaceæ	97	32	33
9. Filices	134	30	22
10. Ranunculaceæ	80	27	34
11. Ericaceæ	89	26	29
12. Cupuliferæ	45	26	58
13. Orchidaceæ	71	24	34
14. Liliaceæ	82	24	29
15. Polygonaceæ	56	23	41
16. Umbelliferæ	63	22	35

This table exhibits better perhaps than any other the special charateristics of the flora. The normal percentage being about 31, we see that in all but five of these sixteen largest orders our flora is in excess of that standard, while it is richest proportionally in the *Cupuliferæ, Rosaceæ,* and *Cruciferæ,* and poorest in the *Filices,* and *Leguminosæ.*

Comparison of Large Genera.

In like manner we may compare the fifteen large genera given in a preceding table.

Genera.	Eastern U. S.	Flora Col.	Per Cent.
1. Carex	180	70	39
2. Aster	63	21	33
3. Panicum	36	19	53
4. Solidago	61	18	30
5. Quercus	38	18	47
6. Polygonum	27	16	59
7. Desmodium	24	14	58
8. Salix	23	14	61
9. Juncus	38	14	37
10. Viola	24	13	54
11. Cyperus	41	12	29
12. Ranunculus	27	11	41
13. Eupatorium	24	11	46
14. Helianthus	27	10	37
15. Asclepias	22	10	45

This table shows that in all the large genera except Solidago and Cyperus, the District of Columbia has more than its full proportion. The genus *Salix* is the one proportionally best represented, while *Polygonum, Desmodium, Panicum* and *Viola*, each exceed 50 per cent. *Quercus, Eupatorium* and *Asclepias* are also well filled out.

As already remarked, it would carry us too far to undertake the systematic comparison of our flora with those of other special localities, even were the data at hand. Few local catalogues are condensed and summarized for this purpose and the labor of doing this is very great. The recently published *Flora of Essex County Massachusetts*, prepared by Mr. John Robinson, however, forms something of an exception to this, and we may directly compare the larger classes and also the orders. The following tables will give an idea of the differences between that flora and our own :

Series, Classes, and Divisions.	Number of Orders.		Number of Genera.		Number of Species and Varieties.	
	Essex County.	Washington.	Essex County.	Washington.	Essex County.	Washington.
Polypetalæ	42	45	155	174	360	356
Gamopetalæ	25	27	158	169	358	389
Total Dichlamydeæ	67	72	313	343	718	745
Monochlamydeæ	18	19	44	47	132	124
Total Dicotyledons	85	91	357	390	850	869
Monocotyledons	17	20	120	112	392	331
Gymnospermæ (Coniferæ)	1	1	7	4	17	7
Total Phænogamia	103	112	484	506	1,259	1,207
Cryptogamia	5	4	20	21	65	42
Total vascular plants	108	116	504	527	1,324	1,249

The sixteen large orders enumerated on page 89 may also be compared with profit:

Large Orders.	Number of Genera.		Number of Species and Varieties.	
	Essex County.	Washington.	Essex County.	Washington.
1. Compositæ	43	53	136	149
2. Gramineæ	50	43	128	110
3. Cyperaceæ	9	10	120	108
4. Leguminosæ	17	24	39	57
5. Rosaceæ	12	15	55	46
6. Labiatæ	22	23	35	42
7. Cruciferæ	14	16	29	33
8. Scrophulariaceæ	14	15	29	32
9. Filices	13	16	40	30
10. Ranunculaceæ	9	7	30	27
11. Ericaceæ	18	11	37	26
12. Cupuliferæ	6	7	16	26
13. Orchidaceæ	13	12	32	24
14. Liliaceæ	18	18	27	24
15. Polygonaceæ	3	3	27	23
16. Umbelliferæ	16	17	20	22

In the flora of Essex County, the orders *Umbelliferæ* (20) and *Cupuliferæ* (16) fall below the lowest of the sixteen for the flora of Washington, (*Umbelliferæ* 22,) while on the other hand the *Caryphyllaceæ* (27,) *Salicaceæ* (23,) and *Naiadaceæ* (28,) not in the list, rise above that number. These orders in the flora of Washington are represented respectively by 19, 19, and 9 species and varieties. With reference to the last named of these orders, however, it may be remarked that the genus *Potamogeton*, which constitutes the greater part of it, has been imperfectly studied here, and will certainly be largely increased when thoroughly known.

The orders in which this flora falls below that of Essex county are: the *Gramineæ*, *Cyperaceæ*, *Rosaceæ*, *Filices*, *Ranunculaceæ*, *Ericaceæ*, *Liliaceæ*, *Orchidaceæ*, and *Polygonaceæ*, nine in all. In the remaining seven orders there is a greater number of species here than there. It is noteworthy that our flora exceeds that of Essex county most in the *Compositæ*, *Leguminosæ*, and *Cupuliferæ*, and next to these in the *Scrophulariaceæ*, *Labiatæ* and *Cruciferæ*. Our comparatively poorest orders are the *Cyperaceæ*, *Rosaceæ*, *Ericaceæ* and *Filices*. Comparing in like manner the fifteen large genera enumerated on page 90 we are able to see still more definitely wherein the two floras differ.

Large Genera.	Number of Species and Varieties.	
	Essex County.	Washington.
1. Carex	71	70
2. Aster	25	21
3. Panicum	14	19
4. Solidago	19	18
5. Quercus	10	18
6. Polygonum	21	16
7. Desmodium	7	14
8. Salix	18	14
9. Juncus	14	14
10. Viola	11	13
11. Cyperus	11	12
12. Ranunculus	13	11
13. Eupatorium	7	11
14. Helianthus	5	10
15. Asclepias	7	10

The total number of species and varieties represented by these fifteen genera is thus considerably larger in the Washington flora (271,) than in that of Essex county, (253;) but whereas they are absolutely the largest genera here, this is not the case there. The genus *Potamogeton* numbers 23 in Mr. Robinson's Catalogue, and the genus *Scirpus* 14, while several others probably exceed ten. Those in the above list falling below ten, the lowest on the Washington list, are *Desmodium* (7,) *Eupatorium* (7,) *Asclepias* (7,) and *Helianthus* (5.) Those in which the Essex flora exceeds the Washington flora are *Carex*, *Aster*, *Solidago*, *Polygonum*, *Salix* and *Ranunculus*, though *Carex*, *Solidago* and *Cyperus* may be regarded as equal in the two floras, and *Juncus* is exactly equal. In *Quercus*, *Desmodium*, *Eupatorium*, *Helianthus* and *Asclepias*, the Essex flora

7

is poor, only amounting in the second and fourth named, to half the number found here.

Relative to the above comparisons in general, it may be remarked first, that the flora of Essex county, Massachusetts, is much more thoroughly and exhaustively elaborated than that of the District of Columbia, lying as it does in the immediate center of botanical activity in this country. This alone is probably sufficient to account for all the difference in the number of species in the two localities, and it will probably be ultimately found that the two floras are very nearly equal. In the second place, if it should be thought that from its intermediate location between the southern and the northern sections of the country, our flora should naturally be the more rich in species, it may be satisfactorily urged on the other hand, that while we have only an inland territory, Essex county has both an inland and a maritime territory. Could our range be extended to embrace even a small extent of sea coast, the number would thereby be very largely increased.

As a final statistical exhibit, more comprehensive in its scope, and from a different point of view, I give below a table in which our local flora is compared not only with the floras above named, but with several others in America. As these several floras not only overlap to a considerable extent, but also differ widely in the total number of plants embraced by each, it is evident a numerical comparison would convey a very imperfect idea of the variety in their essential characteristics. It is therefore necessary to reduce them to a common standard of comparison, which has been done by disregarding the actual numbers and employing only the percentage which each group compared bears to the total for each respective flora. The relations of the several groups to the total vegetation of each flora is thus brought out, and a comparison of the percentages of the same group in the different areas displays in the clearest manner possible the predominance or scantiness of the groups in each flora. Upon this must depend, in so far as botanical statistics can indicate it, the *facies* of each flora, its peculiarities and characteristics. As in previous comparisons, the table is restricted to Phenogamous and vascular Cryptogamous plants, and the same groups are employed, except that the large genera are omitted, while the number of orders is increased to the 23 largest of this flora, which is taken as the basis of comparison, and they are arranged in the order of rank with reference to it.

The several floras compared with the total number of plants embraced in each, are as follows:

1. Flora of Washington and vicinity_____ 1,249
2. Flora of Essex county, Massachusetts_____ 1,324
3. Flora of the State of Illinois __ _____ 1,542
4. Flora of Northeastern United States_____ 2,365
5. Flora of Southeastern United States_____ 2,696
6. Flora of Eastern United States (= 4 + 5)_____ 4,034
7. Plants collected by the Fortieth Parallel Survey _____ 1,254
8. Plants collected by Lieut. Wheeler's Survey _____ 1,535

For the flora of Illinois, (No. 3,) and also for that of the Northern United States, east of the Mississippi, (No. 4,) I have used, without verification, the figures of the *Catalogue of the Plants of Illinois*, 1876, prepared by Mr. Harry N. Patterson, as summarized in the preface. In the former case, the introduced species are included, but the varieties seem to be excluded. In the latter case, as stated by Mr. Patterson, the introduced species are excluded, as are also doubtless the varieties.

For the flora of the Southern United States, east of Mississippi, (No. 5,) which I have compiled from Dr. Chapman's *Flora of the Southern States*, indigenous species are alone taken, in order to make it conform as nearly as possible to the flora of the Northeastern United States, (No. 4.)

The plants collected by the Fortieth Parallel Survey, (No. 7,) and those collected on Lieut. Wheeler's Survey, (No. 8,) are introduced rather as a means of contrasting the Eastern with the Western portions of the continent, than as a proper part of the comparative botanical statistics of this vicinity. The former of these collections was very thoroughly and carefully made by an energetic and experienced botanist, Mr. Sereno Watson, and derives its chief value from this fact. It embraces, however, a territory having a somewhat special character from a botanical point of view, viz: in general terms, the Great Basin between the Rocky Mountains and the Sierra Nevada, and the High Plateaus and mountains immediately adjacent, (Wasatch, Uintas, Sierras,) with a restricted range north and south. The data are taken from the summary of the work prepared by Mr. Watson, and found on page XIV of the Report. The collections embraced in the Report of Lieut. Wheeler's Survey, on the other hand, were made by numerous collectors, some of them amateurs, and were scattered over a very wide extent of western territory, including Colorado, New Mexico, Utah, Arizona and Nevada, and continued through five years of exploration. They may be taken therefore to represent, with some correctness, the general character of our Western Flora, exclusive of the Pacific Coast. The facts given are derived from the "Table of Orders" on page 379. In both cases varieties are excluded.

For the remaining floras compared in the table, (Nos. 1, 2, and 6,) to avoid re-compilation, the data previously used are repeated, species and varieties, including also introduced plants, being employed. As already intimated, however, this difference in the basis of compilation of different floras, applying as it does to the several groups and to the aggregate alike, cannot materially affect the percentages as computed.

The following is the Table of Percentages :

Groups.	Flora of Washington and Vicinity.	Flora of Essex County, Massachusetts.	Flora of the State of Illinois.	Flora of the Northeastern United States.	Flora of the Southeastern United States.	Flora of the total Eastern United States.	Plants collected by the 40th Parallel Survey.	Plants collected by Lieut. Wheeler's Survey.
Polypetalæ _____	28.5	27.2	28.5	26.8	28.9	27.6	35.1	31.9
Gamopetalæ _____	31.1	27.0	32.2	31.6	34.7	32.6	36.0	35.8
Total Dichlamydeæ	59.6	54.2	60.7	58.4	63.6	60.2	71.1	67.7
Monochlamydeæ____	9.9	10.0	9.8	7.9	8.8	8.7	9.8	10.6
Total Dicotyledons	69.5	64.2	70.5	66.3	72.4	68.9	80.9	78.3
Monocotyledons____	26.5	27.6	25.5	29.0	24.3	25.6	16.4	15.7
Gymnosperms _____	0.6	1.3	0.7	0.9	0.7	0.7	1.2	1.3
Total Phænogamia	96.6	95.1	96.7	96.2	97.4	95.2	98.5	95.3
Cryptogamia _____	3.4	4.9	3.3	3.8	2.6	4.8	1.5	4.7
Total vascular plants_	100.0	100.0	100.0	100.0	100.0	100.0	100.0	100.0

Orders.	Flora of Washington and Vicinity.	Flora of Essex County, Massachusetts.	Flora of the State of Illinois.	Flora of the Northern United States.	Flora of the Southern United States.	Flora of the total Eastern United States.	Plants collected by the 40th Parallel Survey.	Plants collected by Lieut. Wheeler's Survey.
1. Compositæ	11.9	10.3	13.0	12.2	13.7	12.3	16.5	16.6
2. Gramineæ	8.9	9.7	7.8	7.5	7.2	7.4	5.4	7.8
3. Cyperaceæ	8.6	9.1	8.5	10.5	8.0	8.9	4.4	3.8
4. Leguminosæ	4.6	2.9	4.7	4.3	6.1	5.2	7.2	8.2
5. Rosaceæ	3.7	4.2	3.2	3.0	2.2	2.6	3.4	2.9
6. Labiatæ	3.4	2.6	2.8	2.2	2.8	3.0	0.9	2.2
7. Cruciferæ	2.6	2.2	2.1	2.0	1.4	1.9	4.4	2.8
8. Scrophulariaceæ	2.6	2.2	2.7	2.3	2.5	2.4	4.5	4.8
9. Filices	2.4	3.0	2.3	2.4	2.1	3.3	1.0	4.3
10. Ranunculaceæ	2.2	2.3	2.7	2.3	1.9	2.0	3.0	2.3
11. Ericaceæ	2.1	2.8	0.9	2.9	2.0	2.2	1.3	0.9
12. Cupuliferæ*	2.1	1.8	1.4	1.5	1.3	1.4	0.4	0.9
13. Liliaceæ	1.9	2.0	2.1	2.4	2.1	2.0	3.0	1.5
14. Orchidaceæ	1.9	2.4	1.8	2.4	1.9	1.7	0.6	0.5
15. Polygonaceæ	1.8	2.0	1.9	1.1	1.5	1.4	4.0	3.2
16. Umbelliferæ	1.8	1.5	1.8	1.7	1.6	1.6	2.4	1.2
17. Caryophyllaceæ	1.5	2.0	1.4	1.5	1.5	1.5	2.2	1.6
18. Salicaceæ	1.5	1.7	1.2	0.8	0.3	0.7	0.9	0.8
19. Onagraceæ	0.9	1.1	1.2	1.2	1.3	1.1	2.3	2.4
20. Saxifragaceæ	0.7	1.0	0.8	1.5	0.9	1.1	2.1	1.4
21. Chenopodiaceæ	0.7	1.3	0.7	0.5	0.5	0.6	2.1	1.5
22. Naiadaceæ	0.7	2.1	1.2	1.2	0.4	1.0	0.7	0.3
23. Polemoniaceæ	0.5	0.1	0.5	0.3	0.5	0.4	3.3	1.8

* Including the Betulaceæ.

Comparisons have already been made of our local flora with that of Essex county, Massachusetts, which contains so nearly the same number of plants. In examining the percentages in the above table, these distinctions are equally manfest. In both divisions of the *Dichlamydeæ*, and also in the Dicotyledons, and the total *Phænogamia*, our flora is richer than that of Essex county, while in the *Monochlamydeæ*, the Monocotyledons, the Gymnosperms, and the Cryptogams, it falls below. In the *Compositæ, Leguminosæ, Labiatæ, Cruciferæ, Scrophulariceæ, Cupuliferæ*, and a few other orders it is in excess, while in the *Gramineæ, Cyperaceæ, Rosaceæ, Filices*, &c., the Essex flora leads.

In the comparison with the flora of the State of Illinois, one is struck by the marked similarity in the position of the groups, notwithstanding the well known differences in the actual species. In the *Gamopetalæ*, and total *Dichlamydea*, as also in the *Monochlamydeæ* the difference is very slight, while in the *Polypetalæ* it disappears entirely. The Dicotyledons are therefore nearly the same, and we find this true also of the Monocotyledons, and the Gymnosperms. Whatever slight variations occur in the above named groups, they are so adjusted as nearly to balance each other, so that when we reach the total *Phænogomia*, we again have substantial unison, which of course is maintained in the *Cryptogamia*.

This harmony is less pronounced in the larger orders, the *Compositæ* being richer, and the *Gramineæ* poorer there than here. In the *Cyperaceæ, Leguminosæ, Scrophulariaceæ,* and *Filices,* the difference is not great, but in the *Rosaceæ, Labiatæ, Cruciferæ,* and *Cupuliferæ,* the Washington flora is decidedly in advance, and in the *Ericaceæ* it is of course in very marked contrast. In the *Orchidaceæ, Polygonaceæ, Umbelliferæ, Caryophyllaceæ,* and *Polemoniaceæ,* there is substantial, or exact identity. In the *Ranunculaceæ, Onagraceæ, Naiadaceæ,* and *Liliaceæ,* besides the *Compositæ* already mentioned, the Illinois flora leads that of Washington. On the whole there is a remarkable similarity in the facies of these two floras, which may be due to their inland situation, with fluriatile areas, and similar position as to latitude. Considering, however, the marked specific peculiarities of the flora of the flat prairies of the West, we would have naturally looked for a corresponding distinctness in the larger groups and orders.

The comparisons of our flora, from this point of view, with those of the Northern and Southern States, east of the Mississippi river, and with these two combined, as represented in the next three columns, proves of the highest interest, and will repay somewhat close inspection. It has often been asked, to what extent the flora of Washington is affected by influences of a peculiarly southern character, and while it has generally been conceded that it belongs clearly to the northern section of the country, many facts, such as those previously set forth, relative to autumnal flowering and early flowering, as well as to the number of species, which exhibit more or less green foliage throughout the winter, combine to give it a decidedly southern aspect. In so far as the method of testing such questions which has been here adopted can be relied upon, this southern leaning on the part of the Washington flora is clearly exhibited in this table. In letting the eye follow columns four and five, the differences are well marked in nearly all the groups, and in most of the large orders. These are what express statistically the essential characteristics of the northern as contrasted with the southern flora. It is also obvious that the figures in column six will, in most cases, express the mean between these two extremes. To obtain the true position of our flora, it is necessary to observe toward which of these extremes it most nearly approaches, and whether it falls on the northern or southern side of the mean established by column six. In instituting this comparison, we perceive at the outset, that in the Polypetalous division, it falls so far on the southern side as to come within four tenths of one per cent. of being identical with the flora of the Southern States. In the *Gamopetalæ*, however, it agrees quite closely with the flora of Northern States, so that in the *Dichlamydeæ* as a whole, it coincides very well with the mean for both sections. The *Monochlamydeæ* agree better with those of the Southern States and the total Dicotyledons fall largely on the southern side of the mean. The Monocotyledons also fall somewhat on the southern side, while the Gymnosperms are below the mean which here corresponds with the southern flora. This leaves the total Phænogams, occupying an intermediate position. The Cryptogams are also very nearly intermediate, though approaching the northern side.

Considering next the relations of the large orders, we find that in the *Compositæ* our flora is northern in aspect. In the *Gramineæ* it is very exceptionally rich, surpassing all the larger areas and approaching that of Essex county, Massachusetts. In the *Cyperaceæ*, which are peculiarly typical for the purpose, on account of being indigenous in all the floras, it does not correspond at all, either with the northern section or with the average of both sections, but does agree very closely with the exceptionally meager representation of the southern flora. The *Leguminosæ* are here northern in aspect, the *Rosaceæ*, like the *Gramineæ*, exceptionally rich, far exceeding either section, as is also the case with the *Labiatæ* and the *Cruciferæ*. The ferns are northern in their degree of representation, as are the *Ranunculaceæ* while the *Ericaceæ* and *Scrophulariaceæ* are southern. The *Cupuliferæ* again are anomalous and tower above all other floras. The *Liliaceæ* are southern, as are also the *Orchidaceæ*. The *Polygonaceæ* are in excess, and in so far southern in aspect, while the *Umbelliferæ*, also in excess, denote a northern inclination. The *Caryophyllaceæ* are remarkable for showing the same percentage in all of the four floras now under comparison. The *Salicaceæ* are largely in excess of every flora compared in the table, except that of Essex county, Massachusetts, while *Onagraceæ* and *Saxifragaceæ* both fall below the normal, the latter, however, showing a southern tendency. The *Naiadaceæ* are southern, as are also the *Polemoniaceæ*, while the *Chenopodiaceæ* are slightly in excess in their degree of representation.

Now, as this locality has been classed as northern, we should not expect to find it occupying an intermediate position, which would place it on the boundary line between the northern and the southern flora, but we should expect to find it agreeing closely with the northern flora, or at least lying midway statistically, as it does geographically, between the dividing line or medium, represented by the total eastern flora and the northern flora. So far is this from being the case, however, that we actually find it occupying a position considerably below the medium line, and between this and the line of the southern flora; a position which would be geographically represented by the latitude of Nashville or Raleigh, or even by Memphis or Chattanooga.

This result is very remarkable, and while the proofs from statistics are, perhaps, not alone to be relied upon, it serves to confirm many facts recorded which have puzzled the observers of the phenomena of the vegetable kingdom in this locality.

The results of the careful comparison of the two remaining columns need not be here summed up, as the reader will readily perceive their general import, and he will not be likely to stop with considering the relations of the local flora with those of the far West, but will probably seek for more general laws governing the vegetation of the eastern and western sections, as we have already done to some extent for the northern and southern sections.

Abundant Species.

It was Humboldt who remarked that of the three great Kingdoms of Nature, the Mineral, the Vegetable, and the Animal, it is the Vegetable which contributes most to give character to a landscape. This is very true, and it is also true, that botanists rarely take account of this fact. The latter are always interested in the relative numbers of species belonging to different Classes, Families, and Genera, rather than to the mere superficial aspect of the vegetation. It is, however, not the number of species, but individuals which give any particular flora its distinguishing characteristics to all but systematic botanists, and it is upon this, that in the main depends the commercial and industrial value of the plant-life of every region of the globe. It is often the omnipresence of a few, or even of a single, abundant species that stamps its peculiar character upon the landscape of a locality. This is to a far greater extent true of many other regions, especially in the far West, than it is of this; the vegetation of the rural surroundings of Washington is of a highly varied character, as much so perhaps as that of any part of the United States. And yet there are comparatively few species, which from their abundance chiefly lend character to the landscape, and really constitute the great bulk of the vegetation. The most prominent, if not actually the most numerous of these, are of course, certain trees and notably several species of oak. Probably the most abundant tree here, as in nearly all parts of the country, is *Quercus alba*, the white oak; but *Q. prunus*, the chestnut oak, *Q. coccinea*, the scarlet oak, *Q. palustris*, the swamp oak, and *Q. falcata*, the Spanish oak, are exceedingly common. The most abundant hickory is *Carya tomentosa*, the mockernut. *Liriodendron tulipifera*, the tulip-tree, often improperly called white poplar, besides being one of the commonest trees, is the true monarch of our forests, often attaining immense size. It is a truly beautiful tree whose ample foliage well warrants the recent apparently successful experiments in introducing it as a shade tree for the streets of the city. Among other common trees may be mentioned the chestnut, (*Castanea vulgaris*, Lam, var· *Americana*, A. D. C., the beech, (*Fagus ferruginea*,) the red maple, (*Acer rubrum*,) the sycamore, (*Platanus occidontalis*,) the red or river birch, (*Betula nigra*,) the white elm, (*Ulmus Americana*,) the sour gum, (*Nyssa multiflora*,) the sweet gum, (*Liquid-amber Styraciflua*,) the scrub pine, (*Pinus inops*,) the pitch pine, (*P. rigida*,) and the yellow pine, (*P. mitis*.)

Of the smaller trees, *Cornus florida*, the flowering dogwood and *Cercis Canadensis*, the red-bud or Judas tree are very abundant, and chiefly conspicuous in the spring from the profusion of their showy blossoms; all three species of sumac are common. *Hamamelis Virginica*, the witch-hazel, and *Virburnum prunifolium* the black haw abound; *Sassafras officinale*, sassafras, *Castania pumila*, the chinquapin and *Juniperus Virginiana*, the red cedar also belong to this class.

Of the smaller shrubby vegetation, we may safely claim as abundant *Cornus sericea*, and *C. alternifolia*, the silky, and the alternate-leaved normal *Viburnum accrifolium*, *V. dentatum*, and *V. nudum*, arrow-woods, *Gaylussacia resinosa*, the high-bush huckleberry, *Vaccinium stamineum*, the deer berry, *V. vacillans* and *V. corymbosum* the blueberries, *Leucothoë racemosa*, *Andromeda Mariana*, the stagger bush, *Kalmia latifolia*, the American laurel, or calico-bush, *Rhododendron nudiflorum*, the purple azalea flower, *Lindera Benzoin*, the spice bush.

Of vines besides three species of ·grape which are abundant, we have *Ampelopsis Virginiana*, the Virginian creeper or American woodbine, *Rhus toxicodendron*, the poison ivy, and *Tecoma radicans*, the trumpet vine, which give great beauty and variety to the scenery.

The most richly represented herbaceous species may be enumerated somewhat in their systematic order. Of *Polypetalæ*, may be mentioned *Ranunculus repens*, *Cimicifuga racemosa*, *Dentaria laciniata*, *Viola cucullata*, *Viola pedata*, var. *bicolor*, and *V. tricolor*, var. *arvensis; Stellaria pubera*, *Cerastium oblongifolium*, *Geranium maculatum*, *Impatiens pallida*, and *I. fulva ; Desmodium nudiflorum*, *D. acuminatum*, and *D. Dillenii ; Vicia Caroliniana*, *Potentilla Canadensis*, *Geum album*, *Saxifraga Virginiensis*, *Oenothera fruticosa*, and *Thaspium barbinode*. In the *Gamopetalæ* before *Compositæ*, we have *Galium aparine*, *Mitchella repens*, *Houstonia purpurea*, and *H. cœrulea*. In the *Compositæ*, the most conspicuous are ; *Vernonia Noveboracense*, *Eupatorium purpureum*, *Liatris graminifolia*, *Aster patens*, *A. ericoides*, *A. simplex* and *A. miser*, *Solidago nemoralis*, *S. Canadensis*, *S. altissima*, and *S. ulmifolia ; Chrysopsis Mariana*, *Ambrosia trifida*, and *A. artemisiæfolia*, (these behaving like introduced weeds ;) *Helianthus divaricatus*, *Actinomeris squarrosa*, *Rudbeckia laciniata*, and *R. fulgida ; Coreopsis verticillata*, *Bidens cernua*, *Verbesina Siegesbeckia*, *Gnaphalium polycephalum*, *Antennaria plantaginifolia*, *Hieracium venosum*, and *H. Gronovii ; Nabalus albus*, and *N. Traseri*, *Lactuca Canadensis*.

The remaining *Gamopetalæ* furnish as abundant species: *Lobelia spicata*, *Chimaphila umbellata*, and *C. maculata ; Veronica officinalis*, and *V. Virginica*, *Gerardia flava*, *Verbena hastata*, and *V. urticifolia ; Pycnanthemum incanum*, and *P. linifolium*, *Collinsonia Canadensis*,

Salvia lyrata, Monarda fistulosa, and *M. punctata; Nepeta glechoma, Brunella vulgaris, Mertensia Virginica, Flox paniculata,* and *P. divaricata; Solanum Carolinense,* and *Asclepias cornuti.*

Of herbaceous *Monochlamydeæ* may be named *Polygonum Virginianum, P. sagittatum,* and *P. dumetorum; Laportea Canadensis, Pilea pumila,* and *Bœmehria cylindrica.*

The *Monocotyledons* give us *Arisœma triphyllum,* the Indian turnip, *Sagittaria variabilis, Aplectrum hyemale, Erythronium Americanum, Luzula campestris, Juncus effusus, Juncus marginatus,* and *Juncus tenuis, Pontederia cordata.*

Of the *Cyperi, C. phymatodes, C. strigosus* and *C. ovularis* are the most common. *Eleocharis obtusa* and *E. palustris; Scirpus pungens, S. atrovirens, S. polyphyllus,* and *S. eriophorum,* are very conspicuous. Of *Carices, C. crinata, C. intumescens,* the various forms of *C. laxiflora, C. platyphylla, C. rosea, C. scoparia, C. squarrosa, C. straminea, C. stricta, C. tentaculata, C. virescens* and *C. vulpinoides,* are the most obtrusive. In the *Gramineæ,* those which most uniformly strike the eye are *Agrostis scabra, Muhlenbergia Mexicana,* and *M. sylvatica, Tricuspis seslerioides, Eatonia Pennsylvanica, Poa pratensis, Poa sylvestris,* and *P. brevifolia,; Eragrostis pectenacea, Festuca nutans, Bromus ciliatus, Elymus Virginicus, Danthonia spicata, Anthoxanthum odoratum, Panicum virgatum, P. latifolium, P. dichotomum,* (with a multitude of forms,) and *P. depauperatum; Andropogon Virginicus,* and *A. scoparius.*

Of ferns *Polypodium vulgare, Pteris aquilina, Adiantum pedatum, Asplenium ebeneum,* and *A. Filix-fœmina; Phegopteris hexagonoptera, Aspidium acrostichoides, A. marginale* and *A. Noveboracense; Osmunda regalis, O. Claytoniana,* and *O. cinnamonea,* are the most constantly met with.

Lycopodium lucidulum is quite common, and *L. complanatum* is very abundant in certain localities.

Besides the above, which are all indigenous to our flora, there are many introduced species in the vicinity of the city, and of cultivation everywhere which manifest here as elsewhere, their characteristic tendency to crowd out other plants and monopolize the soil.

Such are the most general features which the traveler accustomed to observe the vegetable characteristics of localities visited, may expect to see when he pays his respects to the Potomac valley. To

some even this imperfect description might furnish a fair idea of
our vegetable scenery without actually seeing it.

Classification Adopted.

In endeavoring to conform to the latest authoritative decisions
relative to the most natural system of classification, I have followed,
with one exception, the arrangement of the *Genera Plantarum* of
Bentham and Hooker so far as this goes, and the accepted authorities of Europe and America for the remainder.   For the *Gamopetalæ*
after *Compositæ*, however, covered by Prof. Gray's *Synoptical Flora
of North America*, I have followed that work which is substantially
in harmony with the *Genera Plantarum*.   In the arrangement of
the orders, too, for the *Polypetalæ*, Mr. Sereno Watson's *Botanical
Index* has in all cases been conformed to, as also not materially
deviating from the order adopted by Bentham and Hooker.   In the
genera there are numerous discrepancies between the works last
named, and in the majority of these cases the American authorities
have been followed.   For example, Bentham and Hooker have
thrown *Dentaria* into *Cardamine, Elodes* into *Hypericum*, and *Ampelopsis* into *Vitis*, and *Pastinaca* and *Archemora* into *Peucedanum*.
The change of *Spergularia* to *Lepigonum* is adopted, as well as a
few alterations in orthography where the etymology seemed to
demand them, as Pyrus to Pirus and Zanthoxylum to Xanthoxylum.
I have also declined to follow Bentham and Hooker in the changes
which they have made in the terminations of many ordinal names.
The termination *aceæ* is doubtless quite arbitrary in many cases,
and, perhaps, cannot be defended on etymological grounds but as
a strictly ordinal ending it has done good service in placing botanical
nomenclature on a more scientific footing.   It is also true that the
old system does not always employ it, as in some of the largest
orders, *e. g. Cruciferæ, Leguminosæ, Compositæ, Labiatæ;* but whatever changes are made should rather be in the direction of making
it universal than less general.   Bentham and Hooker do not adopt
a universal termination, neither do they abolish the prevailing one,
and they retain it in the majority of cases ; but in certain cases, for
which they doubtless have special reasons, they substitute a different one, and one which is often far less euphonious.   The following are the orders represented in this catalogue in which the ter-

mination *aceæ* is retained by American and altered by English authorities.

American.	English.
Berberidaceæ.	Berberideæ.
Cistaceæ.	Cistineæ.
Violaceæ.	Violarieæ.
Polygalaceæ.	Polygaleæ.
Caryophyllaceæ.	Caryophylleæ.
Portulacaceæ.	Portulaceæ.
Hypericaceæ.	Hypericineæ.
Celastraceæ.	Celastrineæ.
Vitaceæ.	Ampelideæ.
Saxifragaceæ.	Saxifrageæ.
Hamamelaceæ.	Hamamelideæ.
Lythraceæ.	Lythrarieæ.
Onagraceæ.	Onagrariæ.
Passifloraceæ.	Passifloreæ.
Cactaceæ.	Casteæ.
Valerianaceæ.	Valerianeæ.
Asclepiadaceæ.	Asclepiadeæ.
Gentianaceæ.	Gentianeæ.
Borraginaceæ.	Borragineæ.
Scrophulariaceæ.	Scrophularineæ.
Lentibulaceæ.	Lentibularriceæ.
Plantaginaceæ.	Plantagineæ.
Nyctaginaceæ.	Nyctagineæ.
Lauraceæ.	Laurineæ.
Juglandaceæ.	Juglandeæ.
Salicaceæ.	Salicineæ.
Ceratophyllaceæ.	Ceratophylleæ.

On the other hand, the British authorities are followed in uniting the *Saururaceæ* with the *Piperaceæ*, and also in placing the *Parony-chieæ*, reduced to a sub-order under the *Illecebraceæ*; but from the certain relationship of this order with the *Caryophyllaceæ*, it is deemed unnatural to separate these two orders by putting the former into the *Monochlamydeous* division. [See American Naturalist, November, 1878, p. 726.] On the same ground of apparently close relationship, I have followed Bentham and Hooker in abolishing the *Callitrichaceæ*, and placing *Callitriche* in the *Halorageæ*. On the other hand I have followed Gray in retaining the *Lobeliaceæ*, as also in keeping the *Ericaceæ* intact, and not slicing off the *Vacciniaceæ* from one end, and the *Monotropeæ* from the other, as is done in the *Genera Plantarum*.

In the *Gamopetalæ*, before and including *Compositæ*, in the *Mono-chlamydeæ*, and throughout the *Monocotyledons*, serious difficulties occur in consequence of a want of recent systematic works from the American point of view. In nearly all cases the names as well as the arrangement of Gray's Manual, 5th edition, have here been adopted. I have, however, been able to avail myself of a number of recent revisions of genera made by Gray, Watson, and Engel-man* and published in various forms, chiefly in the Proceedings of the American Academy of Arts and Sciences. I have also derived many useful hints from the *Flora of California*, from the botanical reports of the various Western Surveys, from Sargent's Catalogue of the Forest Trees of North America, and from the Flora of Essex county, Massachusetts.

Mr. M. S. Bebb, of Rockford, Illinois, has shown great kindness not only in determining all the uncertain *Salices*, but in generously drawing up a list of them in the order of their nearest natural relationship, which is followed implicitly in the catalogue.

For the Ferns, the magnificent work of Prof. Eaton has furnished everything that could be desired, and is unswervingly adhered to.

The following genera in the *Compositæ* have been changed by Bentham and Hooker, but the new names cannot be adopted until the species have been worked up by American botanists. The old ones are therefore retained with a simple indication of the recent disposition.

> Maruta has been made Anthemis.
> Leucanthemum has been made Chrysanthemum.
> Cacalia has been made Senecio.
> Lappa has been made Arctium.
> Cynthia has been made Krigia.
> Mulgedium has been made Lactuca.
> Nabalus has been made Prenanthes.

---

* While I have gladly adopted the arrangement of the species of *Quercus* decided upon by Dr. Engelman after so careful a study, I cannot do so without recording a gentle protest against the position to which he assigns *Q. palustris.* viz : be-tween *Q. falcata*, and *Q. nigra*, and far removed from *Q. rubra*. Not only the shallow, finely scaled cup, but especially its light colored buds and thin early leaves, as also a special *facies* belonging to its aments and foliage ally this species with *Q. rubra*, and distinguish these two species as a group from all others found in this flora.

Several of these cases are a return to the older names, and whether they will be adopted by American authorities it is impossible to say.

It remains to consider the one deviation above referred to from the prevailing system of botanical classification, which it has been thought proper to make in the subjoined list of plants. This consists in placing the *Gymnosperms*, here represented only by the single order *Coniferæ*, after the *Monocotyledons* and next to the *Cryptogams*.

It is not the proper place here to state the already well known grounds upon which this position of the Gymnosperms has been defended. [See American Naturalist, June, 1878, pp. 359 to 378.] It is sufficient to point out that the correctness of this arrangement was recognized by Adrien de Jussieu, and has been repeatedly maintained by later botanists of eminence. The object in adopting it here, however, is not simply because it seems fully justified by the present known characters of plants, for consistently to do this would also require that the *Polypetalæ* be placed before the *Monochlamydeæ* (in the descending series,) and that numerous other changes be made. So wide a departure from the existing system would seriously detract from the convenience of the work as a practical aid to the local botanist, and aside from the labyrinth of nice and critical points into which it must inevitably lead, it would not be advisable in the present state of botanical literature. But as the position of the *Gymnosperms* is the most glaringly inconsistent of all the defects of the present so-called Natural System, and as the *Coniferæ* are represented here by only four genera and seven species, it is evident that no serious objection could arise on the ground of inconvenience, while at the same time it may serve some useful purpose in directing the minds of botanists who may look over the work to the obvious rationality of this classification, and contribute its mite towards awakening them to the recognition of a truth which, I cannot doubt, must sooner or later find expression in all accepted versions of the true order of nature with respect to the vegetable kingdom.

Common Names.

I am well aware that in recent times it has become more and more the practice among botanists to eschew all common or popular names of plants. This sentiment I share to a great extent and will therefore remark at the outset that the best common name for a plant is always its systematic name, and this should be made a substitute for other popular names wherever and whenever it can be done. In most cases the names of the genera can be employed with entire convenience and safety; and in many cases they are to be defended on the ground of euphony. How much better, for example, the name *Brunella* sounds than either Self-heal, or Heal-all, both of which latter, so far as their meaning goes, express an utter falsehood. Some works professing to give common names frequently repeat the generic name, as such. This has seemed to me both unnecessary and calculated to mislead. It is not done where other accepted common names exist, and thus the implication is that in such cases it is incorrect to use the Latin name. Again it is only done for the commoner species, leaving it to be inferred that there is no popular way of designating the rarer ones. The plan here followed is to regard the genus as the best name to use in all cases, and as *ex officio* the proper common name of every plant, and, therefore, not in need of being repeated in different type as such in any case. But in addition it has been deemed best to give such appropriate or well established common names as can be found. Some scientific men seem disposed to forget that it is the things rather than the names that constitute the objects of scientific study. There is a vast amount of true scientific observation made by mere school-girls and rustics, who do not know the name of the branch of science they are pursuing. A knowledge of a plant by whatever name or by no name at all is scientific knowledge, and the devotees of science should care less for the means than the end which they have in view. Individuals differ in their constitution and character. The sound or sight of a Latin word is sometimes sufficient, in consequence of ineradicable, constitutional or acquired idiosyncrasies, to repel a promising young man, or woman, from the pursuit of a science for which genuine aptitude and fondness exist. For such and other classes, common English names have a true scientific value. The object should be to inspire a love for plants in all who can be made to take an interest in them, and to this end to render the science of Botany attractive by every legitimate means available. In so far, therefore, as English names of plants can be made conducive to this end, they should be employed. Their inadequacy to the true needs of the science in its later stages cannot fail to impress itself upon all who pursue it to any considerable extent.

Finally common names are not wholly without their scientific uses. A few of them have proved more persistent than any of the systematic names, as I have had occasion to observe in examining the *Prodromus Floræ Columbianæ* of 1838, in which difficult work, I must confess, they frequently rendered me efficient aid in determining the identity of plants, which the Latin names used did not reveal.

In appending common names to the plants of this vicinity *The Native Wild Flowers and Ferns of the United States*, by Prof. Thomas Meehan, has been followed in most cases, so far as this work goes, but this of course embraces but a fraction of the entire flora. Most of the remaining names are taken from Gray's Manual of Botany, and from his Synoptical Flora of the United States. In many cases some of the names given which do not seem appropriate are omitted, and in a few cases those given have been slightly changed. A small number of local names given, not found in any book, but in themselves very expressive, have been given, as "curly head" for *Clematis ochroleuca*, &c.; and in a few other cases, names have been assigned to abundant species on the analogy of those given for allied genera or species.

Concluding Remarks.

The foregoing remarks on the value of common names naturally suggest a few general reflections with which our introduction will conclude.

The popularization of science is now a leading theme of scientific men. To accomplish this, certain branches of science must first become a part of liberal culture. The pursuit of fashion, which is usually regarded as productive solely of evil, may be made an agency of good. If it could become as much of a disgrace to be found ignorant of the flora or fauna of one's native place as it now is to be found ignorant of the rules of etiquette or the contents of the last new novel, devotees of Botany and natural history would immediately become legion, and the woods and fields would be incessantly scoured for specimens and objects of scientific interest. It should be the acknowledged work of educationalists to make science fashionable and call to their aid these powerful social sentiments in demanding the recognition of its legitimate claims.

8

Of all the natural sciences, that of Botany is the most easily converted into a branch of culture. Its objects appeal directly to the highest esthetic faculties. It naturally allies itself with the arts of drawing, painting, and sketching, and the deeper the insight into its mysteries the stronger does it appeal to the imagination. Its pursuit, besides being the best possible restorer of lost, and preserver of good health, is a perpetual source of the purest and liveliest pleasure. The companionship of plants, which those who do not know them cannot have, is scarcely second to that of human friends. The botanist is never alone. Wherever he goes he is surrounded by these interesting companions. A source of pure delight even where they are familiarly known to him, unlike those of his own kind, they grow in interest as their acquaintance grows less intimate, and in all his travels they multiply immensely his resources of enjoyment.

The man of science wonders what the unscientific can find to render travel a pleasure, and it must be confessed that a great many tourists of both sexes go at the behest of fashion, and care little more for nature when crossing the Alps than did Julius Cæsar, who could only complain of the bad roads and while away the hours in writing his grammatical treatise, *De Analogia.* While all forms of natural science, so far from paralyzing the esthetic faculties, tend powerfully to quicken them, that of Natural History and especially of Botany awakens such an interest in Nature and her beautiful objects, that those who have once tasted pleasure of this class may well consider other pleasures insipid.

But notwithstanding these attractions which Botany possesses above other sciences, there exists among a small class of scientific men a disposition to look down upon it as lacking scientific dignity, as mere pastime for school-girls or fanatical specialists. This feeling is most obvious among zoölogists, some of whom affect to disdain the more humble forms of life and the simplicity of the tame and stationary plant.

This sentiment, though now happily rare, is natural and really constitutes what there is left of that proud spirit with which man has ever approached the problems of Nature. His first studies disdained even so complicated an organism as man himself, and spent themselves in the pursuit of spiritual entities wholly beyond the sphere of science. Later he deigned to study *mind* detached from body and from matter, still later he attacked some of the higher manifestatious of *life*. Ethics came next, and social organizations; then anthropological questions were opened, and next those of physiology and anatomy, and at last comparative anatomy and structural zoölogy. Phytology brought up the rear and was long confined to the most superficial aspects. It is only in recent times that plants and all the other lowly organisms have begun to receive proper attention, and only since this has been done has there been made any real progress in solving the problem of Biology.

It is a paradox in science that its most complicated forms must first be studied and its simplest forms last, while only through an acquaintance with the latter can a fundamental knowledge be obtained. The history of biological science furnishes many striking illustrations of this truth, the most interesting of which is perhaps to be found in the labors of the two great French savants, Cuvier and Lamarck. The former spent his life and powers in the study of vertebrate zoölogy amid the most complex living organisms. The latter devoted his energies to Botany and to Invertebrate Zoölogy, including the protozoan and protistan kingdoms. The former founded his great theory of types, and his cosmology of successive annihilation and reconstructions of the life of the globe. The latter promulgated his theory of unbroken descent with modification. The conclusions of the former were accepted in his day, and are rejected in ours, those of the latter were rejected in his own lifetime, but now form the very warp of scientific opinion.

Let no botanist, therefore, or person contemplating the study of Botany be deterred by the humble nature of the objects he would cultivate. The humblest flower or coarsest weed may contain lessons of wisdom more profound than can be drawn from the most complicated conditions of life or of mind.

The city of Washington is becoming more and more a center, not only of scientific learning and research, but also of art and every form of liberal culture. Already the public schools have reached out and taken Botany into their curriculum, and we have seen that as a field for the pursuit of this branch of science the environs of the National Capital are in a high degree adapted. Science and culture must go hand in hand. Culture must become more scientific, and science more cultured. Botany has an important part to perform in this work of reconciliation, and there is no good reason why Washington may not become one of the foci from which these influences are to radiate. It has been such reflections as these, aside from the practical needs for such a work, that have encouraged me to persevere in this humble, indeed, but not the less laborious task, and if it shall be found useful to however slight a degree, in promoting these worthy objects, no regrets will arise at having undertaken it.

SUMMARY.

No.	ORDERS.	Genera.	Species.	Varieties.	Species and Varieties.	Introduced Plants.	Woody Plants.	Trees.
1	Ranunculaceæ	7	23	4	27	3	...	...
2	Magnoliaceæ	2	2	...	2	...	2	2
3	Anonaceæ	1	1	...	1	...	1	1
4	Menispermaceæ	1	1	...	1	...	1	...
5	Berberidaceæ	4	4	...	4	1	1	...
6	Nymphæaceæ	3	3	...	3	...	...	...
7	Sarraceniaceæ	1	1	...	1	...	...	...
8	Papaveraceæ	3	3	...	3	2	...	...
9	Fumariaceæ	3	3	...	3	1	...	...
10	Cruciferæ	16	32	1	33	15	...	...
11	Cistaceæ	2	2	...	2	...	...	...
12	Violaceæ	2	9	5	14	...	...	...
13	Polygalaceæ	1	7	...	7	...	...	...
14	Caryophyllaceæ	9	19	...	19	8	...	...
15	Illecebraceæ	2	2	1	3	...	...	...
16	Portulacaceæ	2	2	...	2	1	...	...
17	Hypericaceæ	3	9	...	9	1	.·	...
18	Malvaceæ	4	7	...	7	5	...	...
19	Tiliaceæ	1	1	...	1	...	1	1
20	Linaceæ	1	3	...	3	1	...	...
21	Geraniaceæ	4	9	...	9	3	...	...
22	Rutaceaæ	2	2	...	2	1	2	...
23	Ilicineæ	1	4	...	4	...	4	1
24	Celastraceæ	2	3	1	4	...	4	...
25	Rhamnaceæ	1	2	...	2	...	2	...
26	Vitaceæ	2	6	...	6	...	6	...
27	Sapindaceæ	3	5	...	5	...	5	4
28	Anacardiaceæ	1	6	...	6	...	6	1
29	Leguminosæ	24	55	2	57	13	4	3
30	Rosaceæ	15	43	3	46	12	30	8
31	Saxifragaceæ	8	9	...	9	3	5	...
32	Crassulaceæ	2	3	...	3	...	...	...
33	Droseraceæ	1	1	...	1	...	...	...
34	Hamamelaceæ	2	2	...	2	...	2	1
35	Halorageæ	3	3	...	3	...	...	...
36	Melastomaceæ	1	1	...	1	...	...	...
37	Lythraceæ	4	4	...	4	...	...	...
38	Onagraceæ	6	10	1	11	...	...	...
39	Passifloraceæ	1	2	...	2	1	...	...

SUMMARY.—*Continued.*

No.	ORDERS.	Genera.	Species.	Varieties.	Species and Varieties.	Introduced Plants.	Woody Plants.	Trees.
40	Cucurbitaceæ	1	1	...	1	...	...	...
41	Cactaceæ	1	1	...	1	...	...	...
42	Ficoideæ	1	1	...	1	...	...	...
43	Umbelliferæ	17	22	...	22	2		...
44	Araliaceæ	1	4	...	4	...	1	1
45	Cornaceæ	2	5	...	5	...	5	2
46	Caprifoliaceæ	5	12	...	12	3	10	1
47	Rubiaceæ	5	12	1	13	...	1	...
48	Valerianaceæ	2	4	...	4	1	...	...
49	Dipsaceæ	1	1	...	1	1	...	...
50	Compositæ	53	138	11	149	17	1	...
51	Lobeliaceæ	1	5	...	5	...	...	...
52	Campanulaceæ	2	2	...	2	...	...	...
53	Ericaceæ	11	24	2	26	...	17	2
54	Primulaceæ	5	8	2	10	2	...	...
55	Ebenaceæ	1	1	...	1	...	1	1
56	Oleaceæ	2	4	...	4	...	4	4
57	Apocynaceæ	2	2	1	3	1	...	...
58	Asclepiadaceæ	4	13	1	14	...	...	...
59	Gentianaceæ	4	6	...	6	...	...	...
60	Polemoniaceæ	2	6	...	6	...	...	...
61	Hydrophyllaceæ	3	4	...	4	...	...	...
62	Borraginaceæ	7	12	...	12	3	...	...
63	Convolvulaceæ	3	11	...	11	4	...	...
64	Solanaceæ	5	8	...	8	5	...	...
65	Scrophulariaceæ	15	32	...	32	5	...	...
66	Orobanchaceæ	4	4	...	4	1	...	...
67	Lentibulaceæ	1	2	...	2	...	...	...
68	Bignoniaceæ	2	2	...	2	1	2	1
69	Acanthaceæ	2	3	1	4	...	...	...
70	Verbenaceæ	3	6	...	6	1	...	...
71	Lablatæ	23	41	1	42	10	...	...
72	Plantaginaceæ	1	5	1	6	2	...	...
73	Amarantaceæ	2	5	...	5	4	...	...
74	Chenopodiaceæ	3	7	2	9	7	...	...
75	Phytolaccaceæ	1	1	...	1	...	...	...
76	Polygonaceæ	3	21	2	23	7	...	...
77	Podostemaceæ	1	1	...	1	...	...	...
78	Aristolochiaceæ	2	2	...	2	...	...	...
79	Piperaceæ	1	1	...	1	...	...	...
80	Lauraceæ	2	2	...	2	...	2	1
81	Thymelaceæ	1	1	...	1	...	1	...
82	Santalaceæ	1	1	...	1	...	...	...
83	Loranthaceæ	1	1	...	1	...	1	...
84	Euphorbiaceæ	4	9	...	9	1	...	...
85	Urticaceæ	11	13	...	13	4	6	6
86	Platanaceæ	1	1	...	1	...	1	1
87	Juglandaceæ	2	7	...	7	...	7	7
88	Myricaceæ	1	1	...	1	...	1	...

SUMMARY.—*Continued.*

No.	ORDERS.	Genera.	Species.	Varieties.	Species and Varieties.	Introduced Plants.	Woody Plants.	Trees.
89	Cupuliferæ	7	25	1	26	...	26	23
90	Salicaceæ	2	14	5	19	7	19	6
91	Ceratophyllaceæ	1	1	...	1	...	...	...
92	Araceæ	5	6	...	6	...	...	...
93	Lemnaceæ	1	1	...	1	...	...	...
94	Typhaceæ	2	3	1	4	...	...	...
95	Naiadaceæ	2	9	...	9	...	...	...
96	Alismaceæ	2	3	2	5	...	...	...
97	Hydrocharidaceæ	2	2	...	2	...	...	...
98	Orchidaceæ	12	23	1	24	...	...	...
99	Amaryllidaceæ	1	1	...	1	...	...	...
100	Haemodoraceæ	1	1	...	1	...	...	...
101	Iridaceæ	2	6	...	6	1	...	...
102	Dioscoreaceæ	1	1	...	1	...	...	...
103	Smilaceæ	1	6	...	6	...	4	...
104	Liliaceæ	18	24	...	24	5	...	...
105	Juncaceæ	2	8	7	15	...	...	...
106	Pontederiaceæ	3	3	...	3	...	...	...
107	Commelynaceæ	2	3	...	3	...	...	...
108	Xyridaceæ	1	1	...	1	...	...	...
109	Eriocaulonaceæ	1	1	...	1	...	...	...
110	Cyperaceæ	10	94	14	108	...	...	...
111	Gramineæ	43	104	6	110	26	...	...
112	Coniferæ	4	7	...	7	1	7	7
113	Equisetaceæ	1	2	...	2	...	...	...
114	Filices	16	29	1	30	...	...	...
115	Ophioglossaceæ	2	2	2	4	...	...	...
116	Lycopodiaceæ	2	5	1	6	...	...	...
117	Musci	42	98	...	98	...	...	...
118	Hepaticæ	23	29	...	29	...	...	...
119	Characeæ	2	4	...	4	...	...	...

RECAPITULATION.

Groups.	Orders.	Genera.	Species.	Varieties.	Species and Varieties.	Introduced Plants.	Woody Plants.	Trees.
Polypetalæ _____	45	174	338	18	356	73	83	25
Gamopetalæ _____	27	169	368	21	389	57	36	9
Dichlamydeæ ____	72	343	706	39	745	130	119	34
Monochlamydeæ _____	19	47	114	10	124	30	64	44
Dicotyledones ___	91	390	820	49	869	160	183	78
Monocotyledones _____	20	112	300	31	331	32	4	----
Gymnospermæ _____	1	4	7	----	7	1	7	7
Phænogamia _____	112	506	1,127	89	1,207	193	194	85
Vascular Cryptogamia_	4	21	38	4	42	----	----	----
Vascular Plants __	116	527	1,165	84	1,249	193	194	85
Cellular Cryptogamia__	3	67	131	----	131	----	----	----
Total Flora_____	119	594	1,296	84	1,380	193	194	85

On this communication, Mr C. A. WHITE remarked that he hoped Mr. Ward would be able to furnish some further information concerning the influence exerted upon a flora by the character of the country rocks. It is well known that the constitution of the strata, influencing as it does the character of the soils which cover them, had a further effect upon the native plants growing above them. Thus the granite localities of the east were more favorable to the growth of certain genera, for example, the Ericaceæ than the magnesian limestones of the Mississippi valley. He hoped that Mr. Ward might be able to ascertain how far these influences affected other families of plants.

Mr. POWELL inquired what were the characters or character of plants that had apparently disappeared from the local flora in the comparison of the field results of the present time with those obtained forty or fifty years ago.

Mr. WARD replied that the missing species in the present lists were not confined to any particular family, but were diffused considerably among the several classes.

The Society then adjourned.

193D MEETING.   FEBRUARY 5TH, 1881.

Vice President WELLING in the Chair.

Thirty-eight members present.

The minutes of the last meeting were read and adopted.

A communication was then read by Mr. C. E. DUTTON, on

THE SCENERY OF THE GRAND CANON DISTRICT.

The communication was reserved by the author.

Remarks upon this communication were made by Mr. J. W. POWELL, at the conclusion of which, the Society adjourned.

194TH MEETING.   FEBRUARY 19TH, 1881.

Vice President TAYLOR in the Chair.

Thirty-one members present.

The minutes of the last meeting were read and adopted.

The President announced to the Society the death of Dr. GEORGE A. OTIS. It was moved and carried, that a committee be appointed to prepare suitable resolutions for the action of the Society, relative to the death of Dr. OTIS, and the Chair appointed a committee consisting of Messrs. Antisell, Billings, and Mew.

The first communication for the evening was by Mr. J. E. TODD, of Iowa who had been invited by the General Committee to read a communication on the

QUARTERNARY DEPOSITS OF WESTERN IOWA AND EASTERN
NEBRASKA.

Mr. TODD gave first an account of the three members which compose the Quarternary deposits of the regions in questions. The lowest is in Iowa, and is the boulder-clay consisting of the hard compact clay usually occurring in this formation, with its included rocky glaciated fragments. In central and western Nebraska this clay is wanting. Upon it rests the red clay, a formation of varying thickness, but usually quite thin, rarely exceeding 20 feet. Upon this rests the *loess* which constitutes a subject of special interest. One peculiarity of it is found in the fact, that it overlies the inequalities of the country which existed prior to its disposition; being found upon the old hill tops and slopes, as well as in the valley bottoms, and exhibiting a general "unconformity by erosion." It is composed of exceedingly fine matter without any fragments of rock of notable size, such as pebbles or stones. It contains, however, bands of calcareous concretions in lines which are usually horizontal, and these concretions are often elongated with their longer dimensions vertical. It also holds those calcareous fibres which Richthofen observed in the *loess* deposits of China, and which he believed to be casts of roots of plants. Another interesting occurrence is that of charcoal, which is found in several places in the midst of the deposits in thin bands. The fossils of the loess are the shells of geophilous mollusca.

Mr. Todd held the view that the loess is a post-pliocene lacustrine deposit, and that the region in discussion was in post-glacial time covered with a very large fresh-water lake.

Prof. T. C. Chamberlain, of Wisconsin, being present, and invited to take part in the discussion, remarked that while Mr. Todd had presented in a very able and clear manner the reasons for attributing the loess to the deposit of silt in a lake bottom, he was of opinion that the objections to the acceptance of that view were very great. If such a lake existed over the region in question during quarternary time, it must have been of immense extent. According to the observations of Dr. C. A. White, these deposits extend to the borders of the region which drains immediately into the Mississippi river in Iowa, and they are found nearly as far west as the Rocky Mountains. Their north and south extensions are not accurately known, but they are believed to be very great. Independently of these deposits no evidences of such a lake are now known. Its boundaries are not marked by any known barriers on the east where the configuration of the couutry is now such that no barriers could have existed, unless the region which they should have occupied has undergone remarkable changes of which the nature cannot be specified, and of which no traces exist. To produce such a lake basin very great depressions would be necessay, and there is no evidence known to him which warrants a belief in a former depressed condition of that region sufficient to account for it. Further research may indeed relieve us of some of these difficulties or all of them, but at present they are very great. Prof. Chamberlain could not but commend, however, the earnest and scientific spirit in which Mr. Todd had pursued his valuable investigations.

Mr. O. T. MASON inquired whether the occurrences of charcoal were frequent and bore evidence of human agency.

Mr. TODD replied that charcoal was often met with, and suggested as a possible, though not probable, explanation, that the fragments may have come from some of the recent volcanic regions of the west.

Mr. C. E. DUTTON suggested that there would be little difficulty in finding a natural cause for the occurrence of charcoal, if the surface had been above water at the time it was deposited. There can be little doubt that fires are frequently started in the woods and on the plains of the west by lightning, and it is not at all incredible that they may sometimes arise from spontaneous ignition. Many of the frequent fires in the western mountains occur under circumstances which render it incredible that human agency was involved.

Mr. C. A. WHITE spoke of the great areas over which loess deposits are found. They occur not only in the upper Mississippi valley, but also in the regions of the lower Mississippi. They also occupy a great range of altitudes, some being only a few hundred feet above the level of the sea, others several thousand feet above it. They all seem to be of similar character and constitution. The absence of any barriers is one powerful argument against the existence of a lake, and the great changes of level which would be demanded to establish this hypothesis is another.

The next communication was read by Mr. C. E. DUTTON, on

THE VERMILION CLIFFS AND VALLEY OF THE VIRGEN, IN SOUTHERN UTAH.

The paper was reserved by the author.

At its conclusion the Society adjourned.

195TH MEETING.   MARCH 5TH, 1881.

Vice-President TAYLOR in the Chair.

Twenty-two members present.

The minutes of the last meeting were read and adopted.

The Chair announced the election of Mr. Peter Winfield Lauver to membership in the Society.

The first communication was by Mr. THEODORE GILL on the

PRINCIPLES OF MORPHOLOGY.

Mr. Gill's paper may be found substantially in Johnson's Encyclopœdia, under the title Morphology, which article was written by him.

The second communication was by Mr. MARCUS BAKER on the

BOUNDARY LINE BETWEEN ALASKA AND SIBERIA.

The present boundaries of the territory of Alaska were defined in the treaty of March 30, 1867, whereby Russian America was ceded to the United States. In that treaty the western boundary, or rather so much of it as is here considered, was defined as follows:

"The western limit, within which the territories and dominion conveyed are contained, passes through a point in Behring's Straits on the parallel of sixty-five degrees thirty minutes north latitude, at its intersection by the meridian which passes midway between the island of Krusenstern or Ignalook, and the island of Ratmanoff or Noonarbook, and proceeds due north without limitation into the same Frozen Ocean."

The longitude of this meridian was very properly left out of the treaty on account of its uncertainty. In order to show our knowledge of the subject at the time of the framing of the treaty the following table has been prepared from all known authorities upon the subject down to the present time.

The last three determinations entered in the table, it must be borne in mind, have been made since the treaty was drawn up.

Date.	Longitude.	Authority.
	° ′	
1761	155	Map published by the Imp. Acad. of Sc. of St. Petersb.
1778	169 52	Cook's Atlas.
1802	168 48	Billings.
1822	168 59	Kotzebue.
1827	168 55	Beechey. Br. Adm. Ch. No. 593.
1828	168 54	Lütke's Atlas.
1849	168 57.5	Tebenkoff's Atlas.*
1852	168 54	Russian Hydr. Ch. No. 1455.
1855	168 48	Rogers. U. S. Hyd. Ch. No. 68.
1874	169 04	Russ. Hyd. Ch. No. —.*
1878	168 58	Onatsevich.
1880	168 58	U. S. C. and G. S.

In the case of the two determinations marked with a * the two Diomede Islands are so represented on the chart that the boundary line is tangent to each island.

During the past summer an attempt was made by the party on board the U. S. C. and G. S. Schooner Yukon to make a more careful determination of the longitude of this meridian than had been attempted hitherto. For longitude purposes the party had one pocket and six box chronometers. For determining time the sextant was used, recourse being had to equal altitudes whenever possible.

Plover Bay in Eastern Siberia is about 150 miles to the southward and westward from the Diomede Islands in Behring's Strait. This bay was visited by Prof. Asaph Hall of the U. S. Naval observatory in 1869 for the purpose of observing the total solar eclipse of that year, and, in connection with the eclipse work, Prof. Hall made a careful determination of the longitude of his station. After a careful examination of all the longitude determinations known to exist, and because the facilities for determining the longitude of this place by the Yukon party were not sufficient to improve upon the determination by Prof. Hall, his results have been adopted, and the longitude of the boundary meridian made to depend upon his determination. Before proceeding to give an account of our longitude observations, when near the boundary line, a complete *resumé* of observations for position at Plover Bay, with discussion will be given, this being rendered necessary by the fact that the longitude of the boundary line as well as that of all other points along the Arctic coast and northern part of Behring Sea have been made by us to depend upon Plover Bay.

Previous to 1848 Plover Bay, though an extensive arm of the sea running inland some 20 to 25 miles, appears not to have been known. It is not shown upon any map before 1850. In the period from 1845 to 1848 it seems to have been visited by the whalers. The first information touching it upon which we can lay our hands is the report of Commander Moore to the Admiralty, published in the Nautical Magazine March, 1850. From this it appears that Commander Moore first anchored in Plover Bay, October 17, 1848 Later he moved his vessel, the Plover, farther in, and wintered in the harbor named by him Emma Harbor. He remained in Emma Harbor until June 23, 1849. Concerning the scientific or surveying work accomplished in this period of eight months, he says; "At intervals Mr. Martin, assisted by Mr. Hooper, made a survey of the place in which I had secured the ship for the winter; which, connected with Mr. Martin's and my own observations on the coast to the westward, will, I hope, give a tolerably correct representation of these shores, and when associated with magnetic observations on every attainable point, will, I trust meet their Lordships' approbation."

The results foreshadowed by this report have not come to light. No map or plan of Emma Harbor, or Plover Bay, has been published by the British Admiralty Office, and no statement or account of the observations at Plover Bay, if any were made. General Sabine in his contributions to Terrestial Magnetism No. XIII gives some results which he credits to a MS in the Magnetic Office by Commander Moore, but no *magnetic declination* or *intensities* are given; whence we conclude that no observations, or at least no satisfactory observations, therefor, were taken. A few results for *dip* are given. The geographical position of the station where the dip observations were taken is given by General Sabine, and this position, if due to Commander Moore, is the earliest determination on record of a position for Plover Bay. The position given probably refers to some point near the northern shore of Emma Harbor and is

Latitude, 64° 26′ N.
Longitude, 173 07 W. Gr.

and the observed dip was 75° 10′. From the best existing chart of Plover Bay that we have, it is found that this station is four minutes north, and nine minutes east of the station occupied by the Coast Survey. Whence we find the Coast Survey Astronomical Station to be, according to Commander Moore, approximately in

Latitude, 64° 22′ N.
Longitude, 173 16 W. Gr.

A rough sketch of Plover Bay was made in 1866, by the exploring parties of the Western Union Telegraph Company, and this sketch was published in 1869 by the Coast Survey. The observations were made by Lieut. J. Davison, of the U. S. Revenue Marine Service, and the resulting position is stated to depend upon nine observations referred by a crude triangulation to the mountain Bald Head. The position given by Lieut. Davison for Bald Head is

Latitude, 64° 24′ N.
Longitude, 173 15 W. Gr.

From the best chart extant of Plover Bay, which has been referred to above, and which is one published in 1877 by the Russian Hydrographic Office from surveys by Lieut. Onatsevich, we find Bald Head to be one and a half minutes south and one minute east of the Coast Survey Astronomical Station. Hence, according to Lieut. Davison, the Coast Survey Astronomical Station is in

Latitude,   64°   25.′5 N.

Longitude, 173   16   W. Gr.

As the observations were made, *not* on the mountain, but on the vessel at anchor in the harbor, it seems probable that in transferring the position of the vessel to the mountain some mistake occurred, for the resulting latitude is certainly considerably in error.

The next determination of position at Plover Bay was by Prof. Hall, in 1869, during his visit to this place to observe the total solar eclipse of that year. The latitude was determined with a Pistor and Martin's sextant from observations upon August 3, 4, and 5, by Prof. Hall and Mr. J. A. Rogers. The following table gives the results:

Date.	Latitude.				Observer.	No. of Observations.
	°	′	″	″		
1869, August 3 _____	64	22	22 ±	1.3	Rogers_____	15
" 3 _____			22 ±	1.9	Rogers_____	14 .
" 4 _____			33 ±	1.9	Hall_____	17
" 5 _____			27 ±	1.9	Hall_____	12
" 5 _____			20 ±	2.7	Hall_____	12
Mean adopted _____	64	22	25			70

For determining the longitude Prof. Hall had ten chronometers whose corrections to Greenwich time were determined at the Astronomical Station in the Navy Yard on Mare Island, California, before setting out and returning from Plover Bay. The dates of the time determinations at Mare Island, are June 17–20, and September 18–19, 1869, the interval being 102 days. The time was determined with a small portable transit instrument. With these means Prof. Hall obtained the following results for the longitude of his station in Plover Bay, west from the station at Mare Island.

h.	m.	s.
3	24	21.3
		19.1
		21.3
		21.0
		22.7
		22.2
		22.5
		15.9
		23.0
		21.1

These are the results by each chronometer, and when combined by weights indicated by their probable errors, the resulting longitude is

h.	m.	s.	s.
3	24	21.1 ± 0.36	

Since these results were published, the longitude of San Francisco has been determined by telegraph, and the station upon Mare Island occupied by Prof. Hall geodetically connected with this determination. The resulting longitude of the Mare Island station is, according to Assistant Schott of the Coast Survey,

°	′	″	″
122	16	16 ± 2.2	

or, in time,

h.	m.	s.	s.
8	09	05.07 ± 0.15	

whence we have for the longitude of Prof. Hall's station, at Plover Bay

h.	m.	s.	s.
11	33	26.2 ± 0.4	

For Prof. Hall's station, therefore, we adopt

Latitude, 64° 22′ 25″ N.
Longitude, 173 21 33 ± 6″ W. Gr.

Before leaving Washington we were furnished by Prof. Hall with a memorandum, describing his station from which it appears that no permanent station mark could be left by him, the character of the soil and natives preventing this. We were, therefore, unable to locate the exact spot, but had no difficulty in finding the general locality, and fixing upon a place that must have been within a few metres

of Prof. Hall's station.   Here we erected a pile of boulders as a
beacon, and by means of the telemeter staff, and a small triangulation connected with our azimuth line, we found this beacon to
bear N. 1° 42' 26" E. from our astronomical station, and 462.9
metres distant, or in round numbers 460 metres N. 1° 42' E. of ours;
in arc this is 1" E. and 15" N. of ours.   Applying these reductions
to the position already adopted, we have as the position of our
station, according to Prof. Hall

Latitude,   64°   22'   10"   N.

Longitude, 173   21   32 ± 6" W. Gr.

In 1876 the bay was visited by Lieut. M. L. Onatsevich, of the
Russian Navy in the "*Vsadnik*," and a rough survey made of the
bay with a somewhat detailed survey of the anchorages.   At the
same time astronomical and magnetic observations were made.

In 1877, the Russian Hydrographic Office published several
charts embodying the results of Onatsevich's observations, and
among them, a chart of Port Providence, or "Plover Bay," as it is
usually called by the whalemen.   On this chart it is stated that the
astronomical station of Lieut. Onatsevich is, according to his observations in

Latitude,   64°   21'   37" N.

Longitude, 173   18   30   W. Gr.

In the following year, however, 1878, Lieut. Onatsevich's report
was published, and in this report the position of the astronomical
station is stated to be

Latitude,   64°   21'   55" N.

Longitude, 173   23   54   W. Gr.

the longitude depending upon that of Petropavlovsk, which latter
is taken as 10h. 34m. 37s. or 158° 39' 15" E. from Greenwich.
This last result appears to be the finally corrected one, and is
adopted as Onatsevich's determination.

The station occupied by Lieut. Onatsevich is clearly marked upon
his chart, and as we had this chart with us the place was quite
closely identified, probably within a few feet.   The attempt was
made to have our station identical with his, and consequently no
reduction is necessary.

Recapitulating, therefore, we have the following results for the position of the Coast Survey Astronomical Station at Plover Bay :

Date.	Latitude.			Longitude.			Authority.
	°	′	″	°	′	″	
1848–9 _____	64	22		173	16		Com'r T. E. L. Moore. (?)
1866 _____		25.5			16		Lieut. J. Davison.
Aug., 1869____		22	10		21	32	Prof. A. Hall.
July, 1876____		21	55		23	54	Lieut. M. L. Onatsevich.
Sept., 1880____		21	54	_____			U. S. C. and G. S., by M. Baker.

Discussion of foregoing Table.

It is very doubtful whether the results credited to Commodore Moore were really obtained by him, or whether General Sabine took these values from other sources ; while the results by Lieut. Davison are known to have been of only a very approximate character. The three remaining results for latitude, when we consider that they were made at different times, by different observers, at different stations, and with different instruments and the instruments of a secondary character, show a satisfactory agreement, and we adopt the simple mean for the latitude determination, which is 64° 22′ 00″ and would assign an arbitrary probable error of 6″.

Neglecting the longitude results by Moore and Davison as being of an inferior character, we have the two remaining by Hall and Onatsevich. The determination by Onatsevich is a chronometric one from Petropavlovsk. How the longitude of Petropavlovsk was obtained we are not informed, but we know it was not determined by telegraph. Moreover the longitude adopted by Onatsevich for Petropavlovsk differs by as much as four miles, (4′ 11.7″ = 16.8s) from that adopted by the Russian Hydrographic Office, in 1850, as the basis for their charts of this region, and which determination was the mean of nine different determinations extending from 1779 to 1827. The longitude of Plover Bay based upon Onatsevich's observations and that longitude of Petropavlovsk is 173° 19′ 22″ W. Gr.

It has, therefore seemed best to adopt without change the result of Prof. Hall's observations, not combining it with anything else, viz: 173° 21′ 32″ ± 6″ W. Gr.

9

Our adopted value, therefore, of the geographical position of the Astronomical Station of the U. S. Coast and Geodetic Survey at Plover Bay, Eastern Siberia, is

Latitude, $64°$ $22'$ $00'' \pm 6''$ N.

$$\text{Longitude,} \left\{ \begin{array}{cccc} 173 & 21 & 32 & \pm 6 \\ h. & m. & s. & s. \\ 11 & 33 & 26.1 & \pm 0.4 \end{array} \right\} \text{W. Gr.}$$

One station was marked by driving a piece of whale's rib into the ground and piling rocks around it. Being identical with the station of Lieut. Onatsevich, any one visiting the place will by the aid of that chart readily identify it.

Having completed our investigation of the geographical position of Plover Bay, we proceed to detail our observations for the longitude of the boundary.

The Yukon arrived at Plover Bay at ten in the evening of August 11, 1880. The following day was cloudy in the morning, afterward rained, and later partially cleared up so that we obtained two pairs of equal altitudes of the sun for time, the interval being about three hours. During the afternoon we succeeded in getting four sets of six each of double altitudes of the sun for time. From the equal altitudes the time of local mean noon by the chronometer, was 11h. 18m. 13.9s, and from the double altitude it was 11h. 18m. 14.2s., a very satisfactory agreement. By means of the intervals the probable errors of each of these determinations have been made out. For the equal altitudes it is $\pm$ 1.7s, and for the double altitudes it is $\pm$ 0.30s, values which may be taken as fairly representative of the different conditions under which the observations were made. From these observations the corrections of our chronometers to Greenwich mean time on August 12 were determined.

On August 14, we sailed from Plover Bay to the eastward and northward, cruising along the Arctic coast as far as Point Belcher, and returning thence passed through Behring Strait to Port Clarence, and afterwards returning to Behring Strait made a landing on the southeastern shore of Ratmanoff, or the Big Diomede Island, on September 10. We came to anchor at seven in the morning, about a mile off shore, and sailed away about three in the afternoon. During our stay observations were made for latitude and time, and all the magnetic elements, declination, dip and intensity. Of time observations three sets of six each of double altitudes of the sun were obtained with sextant and artificial horizon. These three sets give as the correction of our "hack," or observing chronometer, to local mean time

$$h. \quad m. \quad s. \quad s.$$
$$+ 1 \quad 03 \quad 26.9 \pm 0.35,$$

this probable error resulting from computing the eighteen observations singly and treating in the usual way. The sky was nearly covered with cumulus clouds, the wind fresh, raw and chilly, and thermometer 39° F. Near noon the sun appeared again for a short time, and nine pointings were obtained for latitude, giving the following results, each depending upon a single observation.

$$65° \quad 44' \quad 54''$$
$$50$$
$$38$$
$$54$$
$$44$$
$$52$$
$$53$$
$$60$$
$$65$$

Mean latitude, 65°   44'   51 $\pm$ 1.''5 N.

Leaving the Diomedes on the afternoon of September 10, we sailed directly for Plover Bay. That night we were stopped by ice, the next day delayed by calms, but on the following day, September 12, we reached our anchorage in Plover Bay a little before noon, just in time to get a good series—39 observations of circummeridian altitudes of the sun for latitude. In the afternoon we obtained a good series of time observations, but the following morning was cloudy. We succeeded, however, in getting four altitudes corresponding to those of the preceding day, thus enabling our time determination to hang upon four pairs of equal altitudes, the epoch being local mean midnight September 12 and 13. The times of local apparent midnight from these four pairs by our "hack" were

$$h. \quad m. \quad s.$$
$$11 \quad 09 \quad 0.2$$
$$1.2$$
$$0.3$$
$$0.7$$

from which the probable error is found to be $\pm$ 0.15s.

For the longitude of our station upon the Big Diomede Island we have, therefore, as follows:

Plover Bay_____1880, Aug. 12, noon _____Chron'r corr'n determined, ± 1.7 s.
Big Diomede Id.,   "   Sept. 10, 8.9 h. a. m.,   "   "   ± 0.35
Plover Bay_____   "   "   12, midnight___   "   "   ± 0.15

By means of the time determinations of August 12 and September 12, the rates of the chronometers are determined and then the Greenwich time determination at Big Diomede Island, September 10, is made to depend upon the determination at Plover Bay, September 12, and the rates of all the chronometers carried back to September 10, a period of 2.64 days.

The resulting longitude by each chronometer is shown in the following table:

Chron'r.	h.	m.	s.
214	11	16	18.3
866			17.9
1131			18.0
1713			19.0
2535			14.7
311			16.6

Chronometer No. 2535 was our "hack," and 311 a sidereal chronometer used in making comparisons. Each had rather large rates, that of 2535 exceeding *nine* seconds, and that of 311 *five* seconds per day. The indiscriminate mean of all is 11h. 16m. 17.4s. Assigning only half weight to chronometer 2535, the longitude resulting is

h.	m.	s.
11	16	17.7

The probable error of the Greenwich time at the Diomedes, based upon the agreement of the chronometer is ± 0.36s.

For the probable error of the longitude, therefore, we have

Probable error of longitude of Plover Bay_____ _____= ± 0.39 s.
Probable error local time determination, Plover Bay, Sept. 12_____= ± 0.15
Probable error local time determination, Diomedes, Sept. 10_____= ± 0.35
Probable error Greenwich time determination, Diomedes, Sept. 10_= ± 0.36

              h.   m.   s.   s.
Resulting longitude adopted, 11   16   17.7 ± 0.65.

The astronomical station of the United States Coast and Geodetic

Survey at the mouth of the ravine, on the southeastern shore of the Big Diomede Island, in Behring Strait, is, therefore, in

Latitude,   65° 44′ 51″   N.
Longitude, 169   04   25 ± 10 ′ W. Gr.

From bearings and angles taken from the astronomical station and from the schooner at anchor, using the distance of the schooner from the station as a base line, together with other bearings taken while in the vicinity of the islands, a sketch of the two islands has been prepared from which it appears that the meridian tangent to the extreme eastern edge of the larger island is 2.1 nautical miles, and the meridian tangent to the extreme western edge of the smaller island is 3.1 nautical miles, east of the astronomical station. The boundary line is to pass midway between these meridians, i. e. the meridian which forms the boundary is 2.6 nautical miles east of the astronomical station.

In latitude 65° 45′, the latitude of the astronomical station, 2.6 nautical miles is equal to 6′ 20″ of longitude, and, deducting this from the longitude of the astronomical station, the longitude of the boundary line is found to be

168° 58′ 05″ W. Gr.

If we assume an uncertainty of one quarter of a nautical mile, equal in this latitude to 37″ of longitude, in thus transferring the position of the station to the boundary line, and this seems to be quite large enough, we have finally as the longitude of the boundary line between Alaska and Eastern Siberia

$$\begin{array}{cccc} ° & ′ & ″ & ″ \\ 168 & 58 & 05 & + \ 38 \end{array}$$

or, in time,

$$\begin{array}{cccc} h. & m. & s. & s. \\ 11 & 15 & 52.3 & \pm \ 2.5 \ \text{W. Gr.} \end{array}$$

ERRATA.

Page 126, line 6 from bottom, *for* " and returning " *read* " and after returning."

For " Behring," *read* " Bering," throughout this article.

196TH MEETING. MARCH 19, 1881.

Vice-President TAYLOR in the Chair.

Thirty members and visitors present.

The minutes of the last meeting were read and adopted.

The communication for the evening was by Mr. J. W. POWELL, on

LIMITATIONS TO THE USE OF SOME ANTHROPOLOGIC DATA.

This paper is published in full in the "Abstract of Transactions of the Anthropological Society of Washington, D. C., for the first year ending January 20, 1880, and the second year ending January 18, 1881."

Remarks upon this communication were made by Messrs. GILL, HARKNESS, WARD, NEWCOMB, and ALVORD.

At the conclusion of the discussion the Society adjourned.

197TH MEETING. APRIL 2D, 1881.

Vice-President TAYLOR in the Chair.

Thirty-nine members and visitors present.

The consideration of the minutes of the last meeting was postponed, the recorder being absent.

Dr. ANTISELL, on behalf of the committee appointed at the last meeting of the Society, reported the following resolution in commemoration of the late Dr. GEORGE A. OTIS:

Resolved, That this Society has heard with profound regret of the untimely death, on the 23d of February last, of Dr. GEORGE A. OTIS, U. S. Army, one of its original founders.

Resolved, That while we deplore the loss of so highly valued an associate and friend, there is some compensation to be found in the reflection that his long and incessant suffering has at last terminated, and that it is gratifying to remember that he was not cut off before his services to science, in his chosen field, had received, as well in Europe as in America, the high appreciation which they so richly merited.

Resolved, That the medical literature, not only of this country but of the world, has sustained by this calamity a loss which can with difficulty be replaced.

A communication was then read by Mr. A. B. JOHNSON on

THE HISTORY OF THE LIGHT HOUSE ESTABLISHMENT OF THE UNITED STATES.

Mr. JOHNSON read from a paper he had prepared for publication elsewhere, on the History of the Light-house Establishment of the United States, tracing its rise and progress from the first beacon which was erected on Point Allerton, entrance to Boston Harbor, in 1673, to the present time. He gave some account of the eight light-houses built by the Colonies; then of twelve built by the General Government prior to 1812, then of the progress of the establishment, under the charge of Mr. Pleasanton, an Auditor of the U. S. Treasury and the Acting Superintendent of the Lights, when the number increased to some three hundred and twenty-five; then of the causes which led to the creation of the provisional Light-House Board, and then of the erection of the permanent Light-House Board, and of the improvements the Board had since made, in all the arts and sciences connected with the erection of the light-houses and the establishment of cognate aids to navigation. Mr. JOHNSON then gave some account of light-house construction and of the different kinds of light-towers, material and style of the structures used, and of the problems solved in deciding on the various subaqueous foundations required. He illustrated his subject by the exhibition of large photographs of such stone light-houses as that on Spectacle Reef, Michigan, of such harbor lights as that on Thimble Shoal, entrance to Hampton Roads, Virginia, such skeleton iron houses on driven piles as that on Fowey Rocks, Florida Reef, and the tripod erected on Paris Island, Port Royal Sound, S. C., and of the remarkable stone light-house recently built on the summit of Tillamook Rock off the coast of Oregon.

Some account was given of the fog-signals used in this country, and a large crayon of the syren, the most powerful fog signal known, was shown.

Mr. JOHNSON spoke of the fact thus noted by Professor Henry: "It frequently happens on a vessel leaving a station that the sound is suddenly lost at a point in its course, and after remaining inaudible some time, is heard again at a greater distance, and is then gradually lost as the distance is further increased." In connection with this he exhibited a chart showing the site of Beaver Tail Light-House on the south point of Conanicut Island, between the two entrances to Narragansett Bay, with Bonnet Point, on which the steamer Rhode Island was wrecked in the fall of 1880, one and one-half miles to the northwest, with Fort Adams three and one-quarter miles to the northeast, and distant one and one-half miles to the southeast. On this chart was indicated the route of a sail boat which had been run to Bonnet Point, thence southerly to near Whale Rock; thence easterly close to Beaver Tail; thence northeasterly to Fort Adams, and thence southeasterly to Newport. On the route followed by the boat, he had indicated by half inch circles, the audibility of the fog-signal in full blast at Beaver Tail, as heard in the boat; the degrees being shown by the various shades; full audibility being indicated by darkening the whole surface of the circle, and complete inaudibility being shown by lack of shading in the circle. In this way it was shown that the observer, an officer of the Navy, found the sound of the fog-signal faint at half a mile from the signal, fainter at three-fourths of a mile off, much louder at a mile, less loud at one and one-eighth miles; he lost the sound entirely at one and one-fourth miles; at one and three-sixteenths miles he heard it faintly, and right under Bonnet Point, one and one-half miles distant, he heard it stronger than he did at one-half mile from the signal. In the run of about one mile from Bonnet Point toward Whale Rock he did not hear the fog-signal at all, and then he heard it faintly, and as he then ran almost toward the signal he lost its sound entirely; when about a half a mile west of the signal he heard its sound quite faintly, and then lost it, not hearing it again till within one-fourth of a mile when he suddenly heard it at its full power and continued to do so on his run to Newport until three-fourths of a mile away, when the sound diminished one-half, and continued so at one mile off and one and one-fourth miles off. At one and one-half miles distance the sound had diminished to about one-fourth of its power; at two miles off he lost it; he did not hear a trace of it at two and one-fourth, two and a half, or two and three-fourths miles distances; but he caught it faintly as he rounded Fort Adams at three miles away, and when he had run another one-fourth of a mile into Newport Harbor he heard it at almost its full power and continued to do so for another quarter of a mile, when he lost it all together.

Mr. JOHNSON called attention to the fact that in the run of this boat, the sound of the fog-signal had ranged from audibility to to inaudibility, and back again, several times; and that while it was lost at a distance of about a mile, it was distinctly, though faintly heard at Bonnet Point, distant one and one-half miles, and that while it was lost completely at two miles off, on the run to Newport, it was picked up at Fort Adams, three miles off, and heard almost at its full power at three and one-fourth and three and one-half miles away.   These records were made by Lieut. Com. F. E. Chadwick, U. S. N., Assistant Light-House Inspector, to ascertain the facts, bearing on the statement that the fog-signal stopped from time to time, made by those who had noticed these intermissions of audibility; and the fact that the fog-signal was in continuous full blast, was noted by his assistant, who remained at Beaver Tail for the purpose.

Mr. JOHNSON stated that this ricocheting of sound, these intervals of audibility, ought to be recognized by the mariner, who should now understand that in sailing toward or from a fog-signal in full blast, he might lose and pick up its sound several times though no apparent object might intervene.   And the mariner now needed that science should deduce the law of this variation in audibility and bring out some instrument which should be to the ears what the mariner's compass is now to the eyes, and also that variations of this instrument yet to be invented, be provided for and corrected as now are the variations of the mariner's compass.   The speaker referred to the benefit the mariner had derived from the promulgation of Professor Henry's theory of the tilting of the sound wave up or down by adverse or favorable winds, and said that by this the sailor had been led to go aloft in the one case and to get as near as possible to the surface of the water in the other, when trying to pick up the sound of a fog-signal.

In this connection Mr. JOHNSON read the following extract from an article entitled *Signaling by Means of Sound, by E. Price-Edwards*, from the [*English*] *Journal of the Society of Arts*:

"In one respect, however, the late Professor Henry, who was at the time chairman of the United States Light-House Board, differred from Dr. Tyndall, viz: in regard to the theory of acoustic clouds, and their resultant aërial echoes.   Professor Henry's explanation of the obstruction of sound in clear weather, and the echoes, is founded upon the asserted existence of upper and lower currents of air, the tilting up of the sound wave, and the reflection of the sounds from the surface of the sea, or the crests of the wave. From this last explanation, Professor Henry seems to have receded before his death."

Mr. JOHNSON said that he called attention to this statement, as he was satisfied that Mr. Price-Edwards had permitted himself to fall into some inaccuracy as to Prof. Henry's action in this matter. It was within Mr. Johnson's personal knowledge that Prof. Henry, up to the last, had considered the theory of the tilting of the sound wave, under certain conditions, as a good working hypothesis. The Professor had it in contemplation when he was called from his labors to attempt the solution of certain of the questions connected with this subject by stationing observers in steamers, around a vessel anchored far enough from shore to be out of reach of land echoes, on which a powerful fog-signal should be in operation, and these observers should be aided by others in captive balloons, who should note simultaneously with them, upon charts and tables previously prepared, not only the audibility of the signal, but all the other data which could be obtained from the action of the thermometer, the hygrometer, and the anemometer, as to the then condition of the atmosphere. When all this information should be tabulated, Professor Henry hoped to deduce something more of the law of the movement of the sound wave under given conditions, and to formulate it for the benefit of the mariner. This was a work which Professor Henry had left to his successors and which the speaker believed they would not neglect.

Mr. JOHNSON then took up an article in the *Annales des Ponts et Chaussés for October*, 1880, *by M. Emile Allard, Inspecteur General des Ponts et Chaussés*, entitled *Comparison de Quelques Dépenses Relative au Service des Phares en France, aux Etats-Unis et en Angleterre*, and called attention to that portion of it in which it was stated in effect, that the lighted coast of the United States measured about 7,500 nautical miles, and that the estimate of the Light-House Board of the expense of maintaining the Light-House Service for the year ending June 30, 1880, was $2,046,500, and that hence the cost to the United States for lighting each nautical mile of its coast was 1,293 francs, while that of France which had twenty-five lights to the one hundred nautical miles [the United States having but about nine lights to that distance] was but 1,155 francs.

Mr. JOHNSON then showed that the length of the lighted coasts of the United States, except those of the Mississippi, Missouri, and Ohio rivers, measured on a ten-mile chord, was 9,959 miles, giving, as his authority, recent statements made on this point by the United States Coast and Geodetic Survey and of the office of the Chief of Engineers of the United States Army; the one as to the length of the ocean, gulf, sound, and bay coast, and of the lighted rivers beside those above named, and the other as to the length of the lighted lake coasts. He then pointed out the natural mistake of M. Allard, in supposing that the amount of the Board's estimates (*Le Budget Annuel du Bureau des Phares*) had been appropriated by Congress for its support; and he showed instead that the appropriations were much less than the estimates, and that, owing to various causes, the appropriations even had not all been expended, so that the actual expenses of maintaining the United States Light-House Establishment for the year ending June 30, 1880, were but $1,943,600 instead of $2,046,500, as M. Allard had inferred. Hence, it followed that, while it costs France 1,155 francs to light each nautical mile of her coast, it costs but 922.7 francs to light each nautical mile of United States coast, instead of 1,293 francs as has been erroneously inferred by M. Allard.

Mr. JOHNSON closed by stating that the Light-House Establishment of the United States had been largely modeled on that of France; that the Light-House Board, while it still hoped to reach the French standard in many things, hardly expected to attain to certain of its economies; that he should not have thought of comparing the cost of the maintenance of the two establishments, but as this comparison had been made in the official French journal, he had thought it well, and due to the science of pharology, to correct the errors which had crept into the calculations of this high officer in the French Light-House Service.

The paper from which Mr. JOHNSON read, and on which he based his remarks, may be found in full in the Annual Appendix for 1880, to be published by the Appletons as Volume XX of the New American Cyclopedia.

Remarks on this paper were made by Messrs. HILGARD and THORNTON A. JENKINS. The latter gave some interesting reminiscences of his early connection with the light-house service.

Mr. TAYLOR said that he wished to emphasize a single point in Mr. Johnson's communication, namely, that referring to Mr. Price-Edwards' statement in regard to the supposed change of view by Prof. Henry as to the explanation of acoustic disturbances, or, at least, as to the source of the ocean echo. The only thing which could give the slightest color to such a supposition was a purely incidental and wholly unimportant suggestion thrown out by Prof. Henry on this subject. Discarding the proposed explanation of the echo by the presence of a hygroscopic flocculence, or invisible acoustic clouds in the air, as quite insufficient in character, as too indefinite in limits, and as too mutable and evanescent in duration, in a mobile atmosphere, to account for so pronounced, distinct, and uniform a phenomenon, Prof. Henry thought, in the absence of any other sufficient surface, that, in view of the large amount of curvature in ordinary sound beams, acoustic waves might be reflected back to the ear from the ocean itself,—probably from the sloping sides of the waves. On having his attention drawn by Prof. Tyndall to the circumstance that the echoes were frequently distinct over a perfectly smooth sea, he admitted that this would invalidate the suggestion of wave crests being concerned in the effect; but he still believed that, with sounds sufficiently powerful to reach considerable distances, it was quite possible for some of the upper sound-beams to be so curved as to be reflected upward from a perfectly level floor, and still to reach an observer's ear placed near the origin of sound. He had also shown that *visible* clouds were quite incompetent to return any sensible echo to the loudest sounds.

So far from receding from his views in regard to the occasions of irregularity in the audibility of sound, in his last Report of the Light-House Board—that for 1877, published but a short time before his death—he announced his previous conclusions as only more confirmed by his later observations; and a summary of these conclusions was also published in the Smithsonian Report for 1877.

The ideas of sound transmission promulgated in popular books and lectures, as derived from class-room experiments, are very inaccurate and misleading when applied to any considerable range of sound travel. Were the medium of sound propagation—the atmosphere—perfectly homogeneous in density, in temperature, and in movement, the beams would indeed travel in sensibly straight lines, but still with a large amount of lateral diffusion bearing no analogy to the diffraction of light. But in distances of several miles—

say from one to ten, as involved in fog-signaling,—it may be said that such conditions of aërial uniformity are *never* present; or in other words that sound beams are never transmitted for any great distance in sensibly straight lines. And hence it is, that after every allowance for lateral deflection, there frequently remain under peculiar circumstances, intermediate points of acoustic darkness, or belts and regions of insulated silence.

The next communication was by Mr. E. B. ELLIOTT, who read from a cablegram from Berlin relative to the Monetary Conference about to meet at Paris, that a fixed legal ratio of value of gold to silver of $15\frac{1}{2}$ to 1, and the unrestricted coinage of both metals at this fixed ratio of value, were to be presented to the Convention as the leading subjects for discussion, and prospective adoption.

The present market ratio is about 18 to 1, the proposed ratio $15\frac{1}{2}$ to 1. Now one ounce of gold and eighteen ounces of silver are equivalents for debt-contracting and debt-paying purposes, but the proposition is that the nations enact that one ounce of gold and $15\frac{1}{2}$ ounces of silver shall be legal equivalents for debt-paying purposes, the option of deciding in which of the two metals the payment shall be reckoned and paid, to be with the person making the payment, or debtor. It is a proposition then to allow the debtor to scale down his debt from 18 to $15\frac{1}{2}$, to scale down his payments 14 per cent. from the existing standard ;—a proposition that the nations in the payment of their public debts may diminish their payments 14 per cent. and also, that the people in their several countries may liquidate their debts, public and private at the same reduced rate, 14 per cent.

The adoption of this scheme of partial repudiation by our own or any other nation would of necessity prove disastrous to its credit.

The ability of our own country to pay its indebtedness is believed to be unsurpassed by any on the face of the globe, but its willingness is questioned, and the sending of a Commission to Europe, and inviting a conference of nations to favorably consider the subject of scaling down the value of the monetary unit of account, must tend to the depression of that credit.

If, with that doubt impending as to our *willingness* to make full payment of our indebtedness, our nation can borrow at the low rate of $3\frac{1}{2}$ or $3\frac{3}{4}$ per cent. per annum, there is reason to believe that, with that doubt dispelled, our bonds can readily be placed on the world's market at the greatly improved rate of 3 per cent. per annum.

To this end it is desirable: (1), that the forced coinage of our legal tender silver dollar (of 412½ grains silver 9-10 fine) be discontinued; (2), that on all future coins and on bullion, be stamped their weight in grammes, and their fineness 9-10; and (3) that an international commission be created whose duty it shall be to periodically (annually or oftener) proclaim, based on the market quotations of the few months immediately preceding the date of the proclamation, the value in gold of an equal weight of silver; and (4) that the metric-stamped coin and bullion at the proclaimed ratio of value, shall each be equally legal tender of payment in unlimited amount, until the issuing of the next periodical proclamation.

This would be true bi-metallism. The adoption of the proposed ratio, 15½, would be silver mono-metallism under the misnomer of bi-metallism.

By the adoption of the true bi-metallic method proposed—*i. e.*, frequent periodical publication of the true market ratio, instead of a single arbitrary proclamation to last for all time—we should stand before the world with our willingness to pay undoubted, and our ability to pay unsurpassed and paramount among the nations, and our national debt could be placed on the market on more favorable terms than that of any other commercial country.

At the conclusion of Mr. Elliott's remarks, the Society adjourned.

198TH MEETING.   APRIL 16, 1881.

The President in the Chair.

Fifty-four members and visitors present.

The minutes of the 196th and 197th meetings were read and adopted.

The Chair announced to the Society the election to membership of Mr. WILLIAM A. DeCAINDRY.

The first communication of the evening was by Mr. ALEXANDER GRAHAM BELL, announcing to the Society, the discovery of

THE SPECTROPHONE.

In a paper read before the American Association for the Advancement of science, last August, I described certain experiments made by Mr. Sumner Tainter and myself, which had resulted in the construction of a "*Photophone*," or apparatus for the production of sound by light;* and it will be my object to-day to describe the progress we have made in the investigation of photophonic phenomena since the date of this communication.

In my Boston paper the discovery was announced, that thin disks of very many different substances *emitted sounds* when exposed to the action of a rapidly-interrupted beam of sunlight. The great variety of material used in these experiments led me to believe that sonorousness under such circumstances would be found to be a general property of all matter.

At that time we had failed to obtain audible effects from masses of the various substances which became sonorous in the condition of thin diaphragms, but this failure was explained upon the supposition that the molecular disturbance produced by the light was chiefly a surface action, and that under the circumstances of the experiments, the vibration had to be transmitted through the mass of the substance in order to affect the ear. It was therefore supposed that, if we could lead to the ear, air that was directly in contact with the illuminated surface, louder sounds might be obtained, and solid masses be found to be as sonorous as thin diaphragms. First experiments made to verify this hypothesis pointed towards success. A beam of sunlight was focussed into one end of an open tube, the ear being placed at the other end. Upon interrupting the beam, a clear, musical tone was heard, the pitch depending upon the frequency of the interruption of the light, and the loudness upon the material composing the tube.

At this stage our experiments were interrupted, as circumstances called me to Europe.

While in Paris a new form of the experiment occurred to my mind, which would not only enable us to investigate the sounds

---

* Proceedings of American Association for the Advancement of Science, Aug. 27th, 1880; see, also, American Journal of Science, vol. xx, p. 305; Journal of the American Electrical Society, vol. iii, p. 3; Journal of the Society of Telegraph Engineers and Electricians, vol. ix, p. 404; Annales de Chimie et de Physique, vol. xxi.

produced by masses, but would also permit us to test the more general proposition that *sonorousness, under the influence of intermittent light, is a property common to all matter.*

The substance to be tested was to be placed in the interior of a transparent vessel made of some material, which (like glass) is transparent to light, but practically opaque to sound.

Under such circumstances the light could get in, but the sound produced by the vibration of the substance could not get out. The audible effects could be studied by placing the ear in communication with the interior of the vessel by means of a hearing tube.

Some preliminary experiments were made in Paris to test this idea, and the results were so promising that they were communicated to the French Academy on the 11th of October, 1880, in a note read for me by Mr. Antoine Breguet.* Shortly afterwards I wrote to Mr. Tainter, suggesting that he should carry on the investigation in America, as circumstances prevented me from doing so myself in Europe. As these experiments seemed to have formed the common starting point for a series of independent researches of the most important character carried on simultaneously in America by Mr. Tainter, and in Europe by M. Mercadier,† Prof. Tyndall,‡ W. E. Rönton,§ and W. H. Preece,‖ I may be permitted to quote from my letter to Mr. Tainter the passage describing the experiments referred to :

"Metropolitan Hotel, Rue Cambon, Paris,
"*Nov.* 2, 1880.

"Dear Mr. Tainter: * * * I have devised a method of producing sounds by the action of an intermittent beam of light from substances that cannot be obtained in the shape of thin diaphragms or in the tubular form ; indeed, the method is specially adapted to testing the generality of the phenomenon we have discovered, as it can be adapted to solids, liquids, and gases.

"Place the substance to be experimented with in a glass test-tube,

---

* *Comptes Rendus,* vol. xcl, p. 595.

† "Notes on Radiophony," *Comptes Rendus,* Dec. 6 and 13, 1880; Feb. 21 and 28, 1881.   See, also, *Journal de Physique,* vol. x, p. 53.

‡ "Action of an Intermittent Beam of Radiant Heat upon Gaseous Matter." *Proc. Royal Society,* Jan. 13, 1881, vol. xxxi, p. 307.

§ "On the tones which arise from the intermittent illumination of a gas."   See *Annalen der Phys. und Chemie,* Jan., 1881, No. 1, p. 155.

‖ "On the conversion of Radiant Energy into Sonorous Vibration." *Proc. Royal Society,* March 10, 1881, vol. xxxi, p. 506.

connect a rubber tube with the mouth of the test-tube, placing the other end of the pipe to the ear. Then focus the intermittent beam upon the substance in the tube. I have tried a large number of substances in this way with great success, although it is extremely difficult to get a glimpse of the sun here, and when it does shine the intensity of the light is not to be compared with that to be obtained in Washington. I got splendid effects from crystals of bichromate of potash, crystals of sulphate of copper, and from tobacco smoke. A whole cigar placed in the test-tube produced a very loud sound. I could not hear anything from plain water, but when the water was discolored with ink a feeble sound was heard. I would suggest that you might repeat these experiments and extend the results," &c., &c.

Upon my return to Washington in the early part of January.* Mr. Tainter communicated to me the results of the experiments he had made in my laboratory during my absence in Europe.

He had commenced by examining the sonorous properties of a vast number of substances enclosed in test-tubes in a simple empirical search for loud effects. He was thus led gradually to the discovery that cotton-wool, worsted, silk, and fibrous materials generally, produced much louder sounds than hard rigid bodies like crystals, or diaphragms such as we had hitherto used.

In order to study the effects under better circumstances he enclosed his materials in a conical cavity in a piece of brass, closed by a flat plate of glass. A brass tube leading into the cavity served for connection with the hearing-tube. When this conical cavity was stuffed with worsted or other fibrous materials the sounds produced were much louder than when a test-tube was employed. This form of receiver is shown in Figure I.

Mr. Tainter next collected silks and worsteds of different colors, and speedily found that the darkest shades produced the best effects. Black worsted especially gave an extremely loud sound.

As white cotton wool had proved itself equal, if not superior, to any other white fibrous material before tried, he was anxious to obtain colored specimens for comparison. Not having any at hand, however, he tried the effect of darkening some cotton-wool with lamp-black. Such a marked reinforcement of the sound resulted that he was induced to try lamp-black alone.

About a teaspoonful of lamp-black was placed in a test-tube and

---

* On the 7th of January.

exposed to an intermittent beam of sunlight. The sound produced was much louder than any heard before.

Upon smoking a piece of plate-glass, and holding it in the intermittent beam with the lamp-black surface towards the sun, the sound produced was loud enough to be heard, with attention, in any part of the room. With the lamp-black surface turned from the sun the sound was much feebler.

Mr. Tainter repeated these experiments for me immediately upon my return to Washington, so that I might verify his results.

Upon smoking the interior of the conical cavity shown in Figure · I, and then exposing it to the intermittent beam, with the glass lid in position as shown, the effect was perfectly startling. The sound was so loud as to be actually painful to an ear placed closely against the end of the hearing-tube.

The sounds, however, were sensibly louder when we placed some smoked wire gauze in the receiver, as illustrated in the drawing, Figure I.

When the beam was thrown into a resonator, the interior of which had been smoked over a lamp, most curious alternations of sound and silence were observed. The interrupting disk was set rotating at a high rate of speed, and was then allowed to come gradually to rest. An extremely feeble musical tone was at first heard, which gradually fell in pitch as the rate of interruption grew less. The loudness of the sound produced varied in the most interesting manner. Minor reinforcements were constantly occurring, which became more and more marked as the true pitch of the resonator was neared. When at last the frequency of interruption corresponded to the frequency of the fundamental of the resonator, the sound produced was so loud that it might have been heard by an audience of hundreds of people.

The effects produced by lamp-black seemed to me to be very extraordinary, especially as I had a distinct recollection of experiments made in the summer of 1880 with smoked diaphragms, in which no such reinforcement was noticed.

Upon examining the records of our past photophonic experiments we found in vol. vii, p. 57, the following note:

"Experiment V.—Mica diaphragm covered with lamp-black on side exposed to light.

"Result: distinct sound about same as without lamp-black.— A. G. B., July 18th, 1880.

" Verified the above, but think it somewhat louder than when used without lamp-black."—*S. T., July 18th*, 1880.

Upon repeating this old experiment we arrived at the same result as that noted. Little if any augmentation of sound resulted from smoking the mica. In this experiment the effect was observed by placing the mica diaphragm against the ear, and also by listening through a hearing-tube, one end of which was closed by the diaphragm. The sound was found to be more audible through the free air when the ear was placed as near to the lamp-black surface as it could be brought without shading it.

At the time of my communication to the American Association I had been unable to satisfy myself that the substances which had become sonorous under the direct influence of intermittent sunlight were capable of reproducing sounds of articulate speech under the action of an undulatory beam from our photophonic transmitter. The difficulty in ascertaining this will be understood by considering that the sounds emitted by thin diaphragms and tubes were so feeble that it was impracticable to produce audible effects from substances in these conditions at any considerable distance away from the transmitter; but it was equally impossible to judge of the effects produced by our articulate transmitter at a short distance away, because the speaker's voice was directly audible through the air. The extremely loud sounds produced from lamp-black have enabled us to demonstrate the feasibility of using this substance in an articulating photophone in place of the electrical receiver formerly employed.

The drawing (Fig. 2) illustrates the mode in which the experiment was conducted. The diaphragm of the transmitter (A) was only 5 centimeters in diameter, the diameter of the receiver (B) was also 5 centimeters, and the distance between the two was 40 meters, or 800 times the diameter of the transmitter diaphragm. We were unable to experiment at greater distances without a heliostat on account of the difficulty of keeping the light steadily directed on the receiver. Words and sentences spoken into the transmitter in a low tone of voice were audibly reproduced by the lamp-black receiver.

In Fig. 3 is shown a mode of interrupting a beam of sunlight for producing distant effects without the use of lenses. Two similarly-perforated disks are employed, one of which is set in rapid rotation, while the other remains stationary. This form of interrupter is also admirably adapted for work with artificial light. The receiver illustrated in the drawing consists of a parabolic reflector, in the focus of which is placed a glass vessel (A) containing lamp-black, or other sensitive substance, and connected with a hearing-tube. The beam of light is interrupted by its passage through the two slotted disks shown at B, and in operating the instrument musical signals like the dots and dashes of the Morse alphabet are produced from the sensitive receiver (A) by slight motions of the mirror(C) about its axis (D.)

In place of the parabolic reflector shown in the figure a conical reflector like that recommended by Prof. Sylvanus Thompson * can be used, in which case a cylindrical glass vessel would be preferable to the flask (A) shown in the figure.

In regard to the sensitive materials that can be employed, our experiments indicate that in the case of solids the physical condition and the color are two conditions that markedly influence the intensity of the sonorous effects. *The loudest sounds are produced from substances in a loose, porous, spongy condition, and from those that have the darkest or most absorbent colors.*

The materials from which the best effects have been produced are cotton-wool, worsted, fibrous materials generally, cork, sponge, platinum and other metals in a spongy condition, and lamp-black.

The loud sounds produced from such substances may perhaps be explained in the following manner: Let us consider, for example, the case of lamp-black—a substance which becomes heated by exposure to rays of all refrangibility. I look upon a mass of this substance as a sort of sponge, with its pores filled with air instead of water. When a beam of sunlight falls upon this mass, the particles of lamp-black are heated, and consequently expand, causing a contraction of the air-spaces or pores among them.

Under these circumstances a pulse of air should be expelled, just as we would squeeze out water from a sponge.

The force with which the air is expelled must be greatly increased by the expansion of the air itself, due to contact with the heated particles of lamp-black. When the light is cut off the converse process takes place. The lamp-black particles cool and contract, thus enlarging the air spaces among them, and the enclosed air also becomes cool. Under these circumstances a partial vacuum should

---

* Phil. Mag., April, 1881, vol. xi, p. 286.

be formed among the particles, and the outside air would then be absorbed, as water is by a sponge when the pressure of the hand is removed.

I imagine that in some such manner as this a wave of condensation is started in the atmosphere each time a beam of sunlight falls upon lamp-black, and a wave of rarefaction is originated when the light is cut off. *We can thus understand how it is that a substance like lamp-black produces intense sonorous vibrations in the surrounding air, while at the same time it communicates a very feeble vibration to the diaphragm or solid bed upon which it rests.*

This curious fact was independently observed in England by Mr. Preece, and it led him to question whether, in our experiments with thin diaphragms, the sound heard was due to the vibration of the disk or (as Prof. Hughes had suggested) to the expansion and contraction of the air in contact with the disk confined in the cavity behind the diaphragm. In his paper read before the Royal Society on the 10th of March, Mr. Preece describes experiments from which he claims to have proved that the effects are wholly due to the vibrations of the confined air, and that the *disks do not vibrate at all.*

I shall briefly state my reasons for disagreeing with him in this conclusion :

1. When an intermittent beam of sunlight is focussed upon a sheet of hard rubber or other material, a musical tone can be heard, not only by placing the ear immediately behind the part receiving the beam, but by placing it against any portion of the sheet, even though this may be a foot or more from the place acted upon by the light.

2. When the beam is thrown upon the diaphragm of a "Blake Transmitter," a loud musical tone is procuced by a telephone connected in the same galvanic circuit with the carbon button, (A,) Fig. 4. Good effects are also produced when the carbon button (A) forms, with the battery, (B,) a portion of the primary circuit of an induction coil, the telephone (C) being placed in the secondary circuit.

In these cases the wooden box and mouth-piece of the transmitter should be removed, so that no air-cavities may be left on either side of the diaphragm.

It is evident, therefore, that in the case of thin disks a real vibration of the diaphragm is caused by the action of the intermittent beam, in-

dependently of any expansion and contraction of the air confined in the cavity behind the diaphragm.

Lord Rayleigh has shown mathematically that a two-and-fro vibration of sufficient amplitude to produce an audible sound would result from a periodical communication and abstraction of heat, and he says: " We may conclude, I think, that there is at present no reason for discarding the obvious explanation that the sounds in question are due to the bending of the plates under unequal heating." (Nature, xxiii, p. 274.) Mr. Preece, however, seeks to prove that the sonorous effects cannot be explained upon this supposition; but his experimental proof is inadequate to support his conclusion. Mr. Preece expected that if Lord Rayleigh's explanation was correct, the expansion and contraction of a thin strip under the influence of an intermittent beam could be caused to open and close a galvanic circuit, so as to produce a musical tone from a telephone in the circuit. But this was an inadequate way to test the point at issue, for Lord Rayleigh has shown (Proc. of Roy. Soc., 1877,) that an audible sound can be produced by a vibration, whose amplitude is *less than a ten-millionth of a centimetre,* and certainly such a vibration as that would not have sufficed to operate a "make-and-break contact" like that used by Mr. Preece. The negative results obtained by him cannot, therefore, be considered conclusive.

The following experiments (devised by Mr. Tainter) have given results decidedly more favorable to the theory of Lord Rayleigh than to that of Mr. Preece:

1. A strip (A) similar to that used in Mr. Preece's experiment was attached firmly to the centre of an iron diaphragm, (B,) as shown in Figure 5, and was then pulled taut at right angles to the plane of the diaphragm. When the intermittent beam was focussed upon the strip (A) a clear musical tone could be heard by applying the ear to the hearing tube (C,)

This seemed to indicate a rapid expansion and contraction of the substance under trial.

But a vibration of the diaphragm (B) would also have resulted if the thin strip (A) had acquired a to-and-fro motion, due either to the direct impact of the beam or to the sudden expansion of the air in contact with the strip.

2. To test whether this had been the case an additional strip (D)

was attached by its central point only to the strip under trial, and was then submitted to the action of the beam, as shown in Fig. 6.

It was presumed that if the vibration of the diaphragm (B) had been due to a *pushing force* acting on the strip (A,) the addition of the strip (D) would not interfere with the effect. But if, on the other hand, it had been due to the longitudinal expansion and contraction of the strip, (A,) the sound would cease, or, at least, be reduced. The beam of light falling upon strip (D) was now interrupted as before by the rapid rotation of a perforated disk, which was allowed to come gradually to rest.

No sound was heard excepting at a certain speed of rotation, when a feeble musical tone became audible.

This result is confirmatory of the first.

The audibility of the effect at a particular rate of interruption suggests the explanation that the strip (D) had a normal rate of vibration of its own.

When the frequency of the interruption of the light corresponded to this, the strip was probably thrown into vibration after the manner of a tuning fork, in which case a to-and-fro vibration would be propagated down its stem or central support to the strip (A.)

This indirectly proves the value of the experiment.

The list of solid substances that have been submitted to experiment in my laboratory is too long to be quoted here, and I shall merely say that we have not yet found one solid body that has failed to become sonorous under proper conditions of experiment.*

Experiments with Liquids.

The sounds produced by liquids are much more difficult to observe than those produced by solids. The high absortive power possessed by most liquids would lead one to expect intense vibrations from the action of intermittent light, but the number of sonorous liquids that have so far been found is extremely limited, and the sounds produced are so feeble as to be heard only by the greatest attention and under the best circumstances of experiment.

---

* Carbon and thin microscopic glass are mentioned in my Boston paper as non-responsive, and powdered chlorate of potash in the communication to the French Academy, (Comtes Rendus, vol. xcl, p. 595.) All these substances have since yielded sounds under more careful conditions of experiment.

In the experiments made in my laboratory a very long test-tube was filled with the liquid under examination, and a flexible rubber-tube was slipped over the mouth far enough down to prevent the possibility of any light reaching the vapor above the surface. Precautions were also taken to prevent reflection from the bottom of the test-tube. An intermittent beam of sunlight was then focussed upon the liquid in the middle portion of the test-tube by means of a lens of large diameter.

Results.

Clear water	No sound audible.
Water discolored by ink	Feeble sound.
Mercury	No sound heard.
Sulphuric ether *	Feeble, but distinct sound.
Ammonia	" "
Ammonia-sulphate of copper	" "
Writing ink	" "
Indigo in sulphuric acid	" "
Chloride of copper *	" "

The liquids distinguished by an asterisk gave the best sounds.

Acoustic vibrations are always much enfeebled in passing from liquids to gases, and it is probable that a form of experiment may be devised which will yield better results by communicating the vibrations of the liquid to the ear through the medium of a solid rod.

Experiments with Gaseous Matter.

On the 29th of November, 1880, I had the pleasure of showing to Prof. Tyndall, in the laboratory of the Royal Institution, the experiments described in the letter to Mr. Tainter from which I have quoted above, and Prof. Tyndall at once expressed the opinion that the sounds were due to rapid changes of temperature in the body submitted to the action of the beam. Finding that no experiments had been made at that time to test the sonorous properties of different gases, he suggested filling one test-tube with the vapor of sulphuric ether, (a good absorbent of heat,) and another with the vapor of bi-sulphide of carbon, (a poor absorbent,) and he predicted that if any sound was heard it would be louder in the former case than in the latter.

The experiment was immediately made, and the result verified the prediction.

Since the publication of the memoirs of Röntgen* and Tyndall†
we have repeated these experiments, and have extended the inquiry
to a number of other gaseous bodies, obtaining in every case similar results to those noted in the memoirs referred to.

The vapors of the following substances were found to be highly
sonorous in the intermittent beam : Water vapor, cõal gas, sulphuric
ether, alchohol, ammonia, amylene, ethyl bromide, diethylamene,
mercury, iodine, and peroxide of nitrogen. The loudest sounds
were obtained from iodine and peroxide of nitrogen.

I have now shown that sounds are produced by the direct action
of intermittent sunlight from substances in every physical condition,
(solids, liquid, and gaseous,) and the probability is therefore very
greatly increased that sonorousness under such circumstances will be
found to be a universal property of matter.

Upon Substitutes for Selenium in Electrical Receivers.

At the time of my communication to the American Association
the loudest effects obtained were produced by the use of selenium,
arranged in a cell of suitable construction, and placed in a galvanic
circuit with a telephone. Upon allowing an intermittent beam of
sunlight to fall upon the selenium a musical tone of great intensity
was produced from the telephone connected with it.

But the selenium was very inconstant in its action. It was rarely, if ever, found to be the case, that two pieces of selenium (even
of the same stick) yielded the same results under identical circumstances of annealing, &c. While in Europe last autumn, Dr. Chi-
chester Bell, of University College, London, suggested to me that
this inconstancy of result might be due to chemical impurities in
the selenium used. Dr. Bell has since visited my laboratory in
Washington, and has made a chemical examination of the various
samples of selenium I had collected from different parts of the
world. As I understand it to be his intention to publish the results
of this analysis very soon, I shall make no further mention of his
investigation than to state that he has found sulphur, iron, lead, and
arsenic in the so-called " selenium," with traces of organic matter ;
that a quantitative examination has revealed the fact that sulphur
constitutes nearly one per cent. of the whole mass ; and that when

---

* Ann. der Phys. und Chem., 1881, No. 1, p. 155.
† Proc. Roy. Soc., vol. xxxi, p. 307.

these impurities are eliminated the selenium appears to be more constant in its action and more sensitive to light.

Prof. W. G. Adams* has shown that tellurium, like selenium, has its electrical resistance affected by light, and we have attempted to utilize this substance in place of selenium. The arrangement of cell (shown in Fig. 7) was constructed for this purpose in the early part of 1880; but we failed at that time to obtain any indications of sensitiveness with a reflecting galvanometer. We have since found, however, that when this tellurium spiral is connected in circuit with a galvanic battery and telephone, and exposed to the action of an intermittent beam of sunlight, a distinct musical tone is produced by the telephone. The audible effect is much increased by placing the tellurium cell with the battery in the primary circuit of an induction coil, and placing the telephone in the secondary circuit.

The enormously high resistance of selenium and the extremely low resistance of tellurium suggested the thought that an alloy of these two substances might possess intermediate electrical properties. We have accordingly mixed together selenium and tellurium in different proportions, and, while we do not feel warranted at the present time in making definite statements concerning the results, I may say that such alloys have proved to be sensitive to the action of light.

It occurred to Mr. Tainter before my return to Washington last January, that the very great molecular disturbance produced in lamp-black by the action of the intermittent sunlight should produce a corresponding disturbance in an electric current passed through it, in which case lamp-black could be employed in place of selenium in an electrical receiver. This has turned out to be the case, and the importance of the discovery is very great, especially when we consider the expense of such rare substances as selenium and tellurium.

The form of lamp-black cell we have found most effective is shown in Fig. 8. Silver is deposited upon a plate of glass, and a zigzag line is then scratched through the film, as shown, dividing the silver surface into two portions insulated from one another, having the form of two combs with interlocking teeth.

Each comb is attached to a screw-cup, so that the cell can be

---

* Proc. Roy. Soc., vol. xxiv, p. 163.

placed in an electrical circuit when required.   The surface is then smoked until a good film of lamp-black is obtained, filling the interstices between the teeth of the silver combs.   When the lamp-black cell is connected with a telephone and galvanic battery, and exposed to the influence of an intermittent beam of sunlight, a loud musical tone is produced by the telephone.   This result seems to be due rather to the physical condition than to the nature of the conducting material employed, as metals in a spongy condition produce similar effects.   For instance, when an electrical current is passed through spongy platinum, while it is exposed to intermittent sunlight, a distinct musical tone is produced by a telephone in the same circuit.   In all such cases the effect is increased by the use of an induction coil; and the sensitive cells can be employed for the reproduction of an articulate speech as well as for the production of musical sounds.

We have also found that loud sounds are produced from lamp-black by passing through it an intermittent electrical current; and that it can be used as a telephonic receiver for the reproduction of articulate speech by electrical means.

A convenient mode of arranging a lamp-black cell for experimental purposes is shown in Fig. 9.   When an intermittent current is passed through the lamp-black, (A,) or when an intermittent beam of sunlight falls upon it through the glass plate B, a loud musical tone can be heard by applying the ear to the hearing-tube C.   When the light and the electrical current act simultaneously, two musical tones are perceived, which produce beats when nearly of the same pitch.   By proper arrangements a complete interference of sound can undoubtedly be produced.

Upon the Measurement of the Sonorous Effects produced by Different Substances.

We have observed that different substances produce sounds of very different intensities under similar circumstances of experiment, and it has appeared to us that very valuable information might be obtained if we could measure the audible effects produced.   For this purpose we have constructed several different forms of apparatus for studying the effects, but as our researches are not yet complete, I shall confine myself to a simple description of some of the forms of apparatus we have devised.

When a beam of light is brought to a focus by means of a lens, the beam diverging from the focal point becomes weaker as the distance increases in a calculable degree. Hence, if we can determine the distances from the focal point at which two different substances emit sounds of equal intensity, we can calculate their relative sonorous powers.

Preliminary experiments were made by Mr. Tainter during my absence in Europe to ascertain the distance from the focal point of a lens at which the sound produced by a substance became inaudible. A few of the results obtained will show the enormous differences existing between the different substances in this respect.

Distance from Focal Point of Lens at which Sounds became Inaudible with Different Substances.

Zinc diaphragm, (polished)--- 1.51 m.
Hard rubber diaphragm-- 1.90 m.
Tin-foil   "   -- 2.00 m.
Telephone   "   (Japanned iron) ----------------------------- 2.15 m.
Zinc   "   (unpolished) ------------------------------- 2.15 m.
White silk,   (In receiver shown in Fig. 1.)--------------------- 3.10 m.
White worsted,   "   "   "   ------------------- 4.01 m.
Yellow worsted,   "   "   "   ------------------- 4.06 m.
Yellow silk,   "   "   "   ------------------- 4.13 m.
White cotton-wool,   "   "   "   ------------------- 4.38 m.
Green silk,   "   "   "   ------------------- 4.52 m.
Blue worsted,   "   "   "   ------------------- 4.69 m.
Purple silk,   "   "   "   ------------------- 4.82 m.
Brown silk,   "   "   "   ------------------- 5.02 m.
Black silk,   "   "   "   ------------------- 5.21 m.
Red silk,   "   "   "   ------------------- 5.24 m.
Black worsted,   "   "   "   ------------------- 6.50 m.
Lamp-black.   In this case the limit of audibility could not be determined on account of want of space.
    Sound perfectly audible at a distance of ---------------------- 10.00 m.

Mr. Tainter was convinced from these experiments that this field of research promised valuable results, and he at once devised an apparatus for studying the effects, which he described to me upon my return from Europe. The apparatus has since been constructed and I take great pleasure in showing it to you to-day.

(1.) A beam of light is received by two similar lenses, (A B, Fig. 10,) which brings the light to a focus on either side of the interrupting disk (C.)   The two substances, whose sonorous powers are to be compared, are placed in the receiving vessels (D E) (so arranged as to expose equal surfaces to the action of the beam) which communicate by flexible tubes (F G) of equal length, with the common hearing-tube (H.)   The receivers (D E) are placed upon slides, which can be moved along the graduated supports (I K.)   The beams of light passing through the interrupting disk (C) are alternately cut off by the swinging of a pendulum, (L.)   Thus a musical tone is produced alternately from the substance in D and from that in E.   One of the receivers is kept at a constant point upon its scale, and the other receiver is moved towards or from the focus of its beam until the ear decides that the sounds produced from D and E are of equal intensity.   The relative positions of the receivers are then noted.

(2.) Another method of investigation is based upon the production of an interference of sound, and the apparatus employed is shown in Fig. 11.   The interrupter consists of a tuning-fork, (A,) which is kept in continuous vibration by means of an electro-magnet, (B.)

A powerful beam of light is brought to a focus between the prongs of the tuning-fork, (A,) and the passage of the beam is more or less obstructed by the vibration of the opaque screens (C D) carried by the prongs of the fork.

As the tuning-fork (A) produces a sound by its own vibration, it is placed at a sufficient distance away to be inaudible through the air, and a system of lenses is employed for the purpose of bringing the undulating beam of light to the receiving lens (E) with as little loss as possible.   The two receivers (F G) are attached to slides (H I) which move upon opposite sides of the axis of the beam, and the receivers are connected by flexible tubes of unequal length (K L) communicating with the common hearing-tube (M.)

The length of the tube (K) is such that the sonorous vibrations from the receivers (F G) reach the common hearing-tube (M) in opposite phases.   Under these circumstances silence is produced when the vibrations in the receivers (F G) are of equal intensity. When the intensities are unequal, a residual effect is perceived.   In operating the instrument the position of the receiver (G) remains constant, and the receiver (F) is moved to or from the focus of the beam until complete silence is produced.   The relative positions of the two receivers are then noted.

(3.) Another mode is as follows: The loudness of a musical tone produced by the action of light is compared with the loudness of a tone of similar pitch produced by electrical means. A rheostat introduced into the circuit enables us to measure the amount of resistance required to render the electrical sound equal in intensity to the other.

(4.) If the tuning-fork (A) in Fig. 11 is thrown into vibration by an undulatory instead of an intermittent current passed through the electro-magnet, (B,) it is probable that a musical tone, electrically produced in the receiver (F) by the action of the same current, would be found capable of extinguishing the effect produced in the receiver (G) by the action of the undulatory beam of light, in which case it should be possible to establish an acoustic balance between the effects produced by light and electricity by introducing sufficient resistance into the electric circuit.

Upon the Nature of the Rays that Produce Sonorous Effects in Different Substances.

In my paper read before the American Association last August and in the present paper I have used the word "light" in its usual rather than its scientific sense, and I have not hitherto attempted to discriminate the effects produced by the different constituents of ordinary light, the thermal, luminous, and actinic rays. I find, however, that the adoption of the word "photophone" by Mr. Tainter and myself has led to the assumption that we belived the audible effects discovered by us to be due entirely to the action of luminous rays. The meaning we have uniformly attached to the words "photophone" and "light" will be obvious from the following passage, quoted from my Boston paper:

"Although effects are produced as above shown by forms of radiant energy, which are invisible, we have named the apparatus for the production and reproduction of sound in this way the 'photophone' *because an ordinary beam of light contains the rays which are operative.*"

To avoid in future any misunderstanding upon this point we have decided to adopt the term "*radiophone,*" proposed by Mr. Mercadier, as a general term signifying an apparatus for the production of sound by any form of radiant energy, limiting the words *thermophone, photophone,* and *actinophone* to apparatus for the production of sound by thermal, luminous, or actinic rays respectively.

M. Mercadier, in the course of his researches in radiophony, passed an intermittent beam from an electric lamp through a prism, and then examined the audible effects produced in different parts of the spectrum. (*Comptes Rendus*, Dec. 6th, 1880.)

We have repeated this experiment, using the sun as our source of radiation, and have obtained results somewhat different from those noted by M. Mercadier.

(1.) A beam of sunlight was reflected from a heliostat (A, Fig. 12) through an achromatic lens, (B,) so as to form an image of the sun upon the slit (C.)

The beam then passed through another achromatic lens (D) and through a bisulphide of carbon prism, (E,) forming a spectrum of great intensity, which, when focused upon a screen, was found to be sufficiently pure to show the principal absorption lines of the solar spectrum.

The disk interrupter (F) was then turned with sufficient rapidity to produce from five to six hundred interruptions of the light per second, and the spectrum was explored with the receiver, (G,) which was so arranged that the lamp-black surface exposed was limited by a slit, as shown.

Under these circumstances sounds were obtained in every part of the visible spectrum, excepting the extreme half of the violet, as well as in the ultra-red. A continuous increase in the loudness of the sound was observed upon moving the receiver (G) gradually from the violet into the ultra-red. The point of maximum sound lay very far out in the ultra-red. Beyond this point the sound began to increase, and then stopped so suddenly that a very slight motion of the receiver (G) made all the difference between almost maximum sound and complete silence.[*]

(2.) The lamp-blacked wire gauze was then removed and the interior of the receiver (G) was filled with red worsted. Upon exploring the spectrum as before, entirely different results were obtained. The maximum effect was produced in the green at that part where the red worsted appeared to be black. On either side of this point the sound gradually died away, becoming inaudible on the one side in the middle of the indigo, and on the other at a short distance outside the edge of the red.

---

[*] The results obtained in this and subsequent experiments are shown in a tabulated form in Fig. 14.

(3.) Upon substituting green silk for red worsted, the limits of audition appeared to be the middle of the blue and a point a short distance out in the ultra-red. Maximum in the red.

(4.) Some hard-rubber shavings were now placed in the receiver (G.) The limits of audibility appeared to be on the one hand the junction of the green and blue, and on the other the outside edge of the red. Maximum in the yellow. Mr. Tainter thought he could hear a little way into the ultra-red, and to his ear the maximum was about the junction of the red and orange.

(5.) A test-tube containing the vapor of sulphuric ether was then substituted for the receiver (G.) Commencing at the violent end the test-tube was gradually moved down the spectrum and out into the ultra-red without audible effect, but when a certain point far out in the ultra-red was reached, a distinct musical tone suddenly made its appearance, which disappeared as suddenly on moving the test-tube a very little further on.

(6.) Upon exploring the spectrum with a test-tube containing the vapor of iodine, the limits of audibility appeared to be the middle of the red and the junction of the blue and indigo. Maximum in the green.

(7.) A test-tube containing peroxide of nitrogen was substituted for that containing iodine. Distinct sounds were obtained in all parts of the visible spectrum, but no sounds were observed in the ultra-red. The maximum effect seemed to me to be in the blue. The sounds were well marked in all parts of the violet, and I even fancied that the audible effect extended a little way into the ultra-violet, but of this I cannot be certain. Upon examining the absorption spectrum of peroxide of nitrogen it was at once observed that the maximum sound was produced in that part of the spectrum where the greatest number of absorption lines made their appearance.

(8.) The spectrum was now explored by a selenium cell, and the audible effects were observed by means of a telephone in the same galvanic circuit with the cell. The maximum effect was produced in the red about its junction with the orange. The audible effect extended a little way into the ultra-red on the one hand and up as high as the middle of the violet on the other.

Although the experiments so far made can only be considered as preliminary to others of a more refined nature, I think we are warranted in concluding that *the nature of the rays that produce sonorous effects in different substances depends upon the nature of the substances that are exposed to the beam, and that the sounds are in every case due to those rays of the spectrum that are absorbed by the body.*

The Spectrophone.

Our experiments upon the range of audibility of different substances in the spectrum have led us to the construction of a new instrument for use in spectrum analysis. The eye-piece of a spectroscope is removed, and sensitive substances are placed in the focal point of the instrument behind an opaque diaphragm containing a slit. These substances are put in communication with the ear by means of a hearing-tube, and thus the instrument is converted into a veritable "spectrophone," like that shown in Fig. 13.

Suppose we smoke the interior of our spectrophone receiver, and fill the cavity with peroxide of nitrogen gas. We have then a combination that gives us good sounds in all parts of the spectrum, (visible and invisible,) except the ultra-violet. Now, pass a rapidly-interrupted beam of light through some substance whose absorption spectrum is to be investigated, and bands of sound and silence are observed upon exploring the spectrum, the silent positions corresponding to the absorption bands. Of course, the ear cannot for one moment compete with the eye in the examination of the visible part of the spectrum ; but in the invisible part beyond the red, where the eye is useless, the ear is invaluable. In working in this region of the spectrum, lamp-black alone may be used in the spectrophonic receiver. Indeed, the sounds produced by this substance in the ultra-red are so well marked as to constitute our instrument a most reliable and convenient substitute for the thermo-pile. A few experiments that have been made may be interesting.

(1.) The interrupted beam was filtered through a saturated solution of alum.

Result: The range of audibility in the ultra-red was slightly reduced by the absorption of a narrow band of the rays of lowest refrangibility. The sounds in the visible part of the spectrum seemed to be unaffected.

(2.) A thin sheet of hard rubber was interposed in the path of the beam.

Result: Well-marked sounds in every part of the ultra-red. No

11

sounds in the visible part of the spectrum, excepting the extreme half of the red.

These experiments reveal the cause of the curious fact alluded to in my paper read before the American Association last August— that sounds were heard from selenium when the beam was filtered through both hard rubber and alum at the same time. (See table of results in Fig. 14.)

(3.) A solution of ammonia-sulphate of copper was tried.

Result: When placed in the path of the beam the spectrum disappeared, with the exception of the blue and violet end. To the eye the spectrum was thus reduced to a single broad band of blue-violet light. To the ear, however, the spectrum revealed itself as two bands of sound with a broad space of silence between. The invisible rays transmitted constituted a narrow band just outside the red.

I think I have said enough to convince you of the value of this new method of examination, but I do not wish you to understand that we look upon our results as by any means complete. It is often more interesting to observe the first totterings of a child than to watch the firm tread of a full-grown man, and I feel that *our* first footsteps in this new field of science may have more of interest to you than the fuller results of mature research. This must be my excuse for having dwelt so long upon the details of incomplete experiments.

I recognize the fact that the spectrophone must ever remain a mere adjunct to the spectroscope, but I anticipate that it has a wide and independent field of usefulness in the investigation of absorption spectra in the ultra-red.

Mr. WM. B. TAYLOR inquired whether the sounds obtained from the two absorpion bands of the ammonia-sulphate of copper were octaves of each other. Mr. BELL replied that this matter had not as yet been investigated.

Prof. WILLIAM B. ROGERS, President of the National Academy of Sciences, being present as an invited guest, paid a high tribute to Mr. Bell upon the very great interest and high scientific value of the discovery just announced.

The next communication was by Mr. G. BROWN GOODE on the

SWORD-FISH AND ITS ALLIES.

This paper will be found published in full in the Annual Report of the United States Fish Commission for the year 1880.

At the conclusion of Mr. GOODE's paper the Society adjourned.

199TH MEETING.   APRIL 30, 1881.

The President in the chair.

Forty-eight members present.

The recorder of the minutes of the last meeting being absent their consideration was postponed.

Mr. W. H. DALL made a communication on

RECENT DISCOVERIES IN ALASKA NORTH OF BEHRING STRAIT,

in which he alluded to the investigations carried on by the U. S. R. S. Corwin, Capt. Hooper, during the summer of 1880, including meteorology, sea temperatures and currents, as well as the investigation of the coal mines near Cape Lisburne. He described some observations made by the U. S. Coast Survey party under his charge in the same region and season, on board the U. S. S. Yukon. The migration of the Asiatic Eskimo; the sources of the warm waters of the eastern half of Behring Strait in Kotzebue and Norton Sound waters, moved by the tidal and river flow; the existence of a supposed new species of sheep allied to the Rocky Mountain bighorn (*Ovis montana*) in the east Siberian peninsula, and the character of Arctic vegetations were spoken of. Reasons for doubting the truth of the account of an alleged landing on Wrangell Land, in 1866, described in the Bremen Geographical Society's publication by a Capt. Dallmann were brought forward, and it was pointed out that the existence of Plover Island, of Siberian musk-oxen, and of certain conditions of the ice alleged by Dallmann, were in conflict with all that is definitely known by scientific men of those matters.

Remarks upon this paper were made by Messrs. ANTISELL, WHITE, FARQUHAR, HARKNESS, ALVORD, MASON, HAZEN, WELLING, ABBE, BESSELS, and GILL.

Mr. J. S. BILLINGS commenced a paper on Mortality Statistics of the Tenth Census, but at the usual hour of adjournment it was interrupted, to be resumed at the following meeting.

The Society then adjourned.

200TH MEETING.   MAY 14, 1881.

The President in the Chair.

Thirty-six members present.

The minutes of the last two meetings were read and adopted.

The first communication of the evening was the continuation by Mr. J. S. BILLINGS of his remarks upon

MORTALITY STATISTICS OF THE TENTH CENSUS.

[Abstract.]

Mr. J. S. BILLINGS described the methods used in the Tenth Census to secure completeness and accuracy in the returns of mortality. The Superintendent of the Census sought to secure the aid of the physicians of the country, and for this purpose sent to each a small blank book, each leaf of which was arranged to record the facts connected with a single death. 70,306 such books were issued, and 24,057 returned at the end of the census year. The data from these books were compiled by causes of death, age, and sex, and the slips were then used to complete the enumerator's schedules. The total number of deaths reported from all sources for the census year will be a little over 800,000, or about 16 per 1,000 of living population, being an improvement in completeness over previous censuses. The results of the attempt to record the number sick on the day of the census are not very satisfactory, and it is feared they will be too incomplete to be used. Taking the schedules for the State of Rhode Island, which are believed to be the most complete, it is found that the number reported sick on the 30th of June was 11.18 per 1,000 of the whole population.

It is usual to estimate two years of sickness to each death, which would make the number constantly sick range from 30 to 40 per 1,000. In the army for five years the proportion was 43 per 1,000.

It seems probable that, while the proportion of sick shown by the Rhode Island count is too low, it is more nearly correct than any other data which we possess.

Mr. BILLINGS continued his remarks upon the Methods of the Tenth Census, and described the methods of compiling the mortality statistics and the forms of tables to be used. The importance of these forms is greater than usual since they will probably serve to a certain extent as models for the State Censuses of 1885. The want of uniformity in tables of mortality was shown by a chart in which the various forms were compared. The various items given in a return of death, viz., sex, age, color, civil condition, nativity, parentage, occupation, month of death, locality and cause of death, were commented on, and it was shown that to present all these facts in their various relations, would require several hundred quarto volumes. A selection, therefore, becomes necessary. The relative value of giving the causes of death in detail is very much less in tables to be prepared from the enumerator's schedules than in those prepared from the returns of a system of registration where the cause of death in each case has been certified to by a physician.

The importance of a proper tabulation by locality is very great, and a certain amount of data should be given by counties. A form of mortality return by counties was shown and explained. The distinction between nativity and race or parentage was explained, and great importance attached to the giving the parentage as fully as possible in the present census.

The modes of compiling by schedule sheets, by cards, and by tallying machines were then explained. The subject of life tables for the United States was briefly discussed—the ground being taken that such a table for the whole country would have little or no practical value, and that life tables by States would be much more desirable and important.

Remarks were made on this paper by Messrs. MASON, ANTISELL, TONER, and HARKNESS.

The communication was followed by one from Mr. S. C. BUSEY, on the

RELATION OF METEOROLOGICAL CONDITIONS TO THE SUMMER
DIARRHŒAL DISEASES.

[Abstract. The paper will be found in Vol. 32, Transactions American Medical Association.]

An analysis of the mortality statistics of these diseases leads to the following conclusions:

1. Diarrhœal diseases are far more destructive to infants than to adults.

2. They prevail almost exclusively during the warmest months of the year.

3. They are more prevalent in the region of this country north of the north line of the Gulf States and east of the Rocky Mountains.

The first two conclusions are universally admitted; the third is not so generally recognized.

Two additional propositions are suggested:

1. These diseases occur in groups, when the cases rapidly multiply during successive days for a week or fortnight, followed by an interval during which few or no cases occur.

2. These groups correspond with waves of continuous high temperature during day and night, which spread, at shorter or longer intervals during the summer months, over the northern climatic belt of this country, lasting from three to fourteen days, and varying in intensity at different times and in different years.

The first of these propositions cannot be established, because of the absence of statistical data relating to the beginning of the initial symptoms of the diseases; the second is proven by data supplied by the Signal Service Bureau. A comparison of these data with the mortality statistics shows:

1. That the month of July is the hottest and sickliest month of the year, most conducive to bowel affections, and most fatal to children under five years of age.

2. The epidemics of bowel affections of children, incident to the summer season, have their beginning nearly simultaneously with the first exacerbation of heat, which usually occurs in the latter half of June; and the maximum daily mortalities more frequently correspond with the maximum temperatures, which occur in periods of three or more days, at longer or shorter intervals during the summer months.

3. With the usual lowering of temperature and absence of ex-

cessive heat periods, which occur after the middle of August, the daily mortality declines.

4. The detrimental influence of summer temperature is intensified by sudden and acute elevations and falls.

5. Children under one year of age are most numerously and seriously affected.

Heat exhibits its deleterious influence in another and very important relation. It is one of the many conditions which, in conjunction, make up a season. A comparison of the statistics of the weekly mortality from diarrhœal diseases in the principal cities of the country grouped according to latitude, will exhibit the gradual increase of these diseases with the gradual advance of the summer solstice northward until it reaches its maximum during the period when all the elements which complete the season of summer are in their fullest activity; also a gradual decline with the return of the winter season.

The total movement of the wind is, perhaps, a more important influence than is generally believed. A comparison of the mortality data with the records of the monthly measurement of the wind, supplied by the Signal Service Bureau for the years 1875, 1876, 1877, 1878, 1879, and 1880, shows:

1. July is the month of greatest mortality and least movement of the wind.

2. The nearer the monthly movements of the wind approach uniformity, the less the mortality for summer diarrhœas.

3. Equality of climate corresponds with uniformity of and moderate or small movements of wind, and small mortalities.

4. Wide ranges of temperature correspond with large movements of wind and high mortalities from diarrhœal diseases.

5. Weekly mortalities from diarrhœal disease increase correspondingly with advance of the summer solstice northward, increasing and greater range of temperature, and larger and more fluctuating movements of wind.

Relative saturation of the air bears no constant relation to mortalities. Moisture in relative excess to the heat of an impure and stagnant atmosphere is the condition which supplies the most satisfactory explanation of its detrimental influence.

Remarks were made upon this paper by Messrs. HARKNESS, BILLINGS, and WOODWARD.

At the conclusion of this discussion the Society adjourned.

201ST MEETING.   MAY 28, 1881.

The President in the Chair.

Thirty-four members present.

The minutes of the last meeting were read and adopted.

The first communication was by Mr. D. P. TODD on

THE SOLAR PARALLAX AS DERIVED FROM THE AMERICAN PHOTO-GRAPHS OF THE TRANSIT OF VENUS, 1874, DECEMBER 8-9.

In the volume of observations of the transit of Venus recently issued, the photographs are presented in very nearly the form of equations of conditions involving the corrections of the relative right ascension and declination of the sun and Venus, and the correction of the adopted value of the solar parallax. The total number of photographs is 213, of which 84 were obtained at stations in the northern hemisphere, and 129 in the southern.

Every photograph gives one equation of condition in distance, s, of the form

$$0 = a\,\delta A + b\,\delta D + c\,\delta\omega - (0. - C.)$$

The normal equations in s are—

$$+ 23.99\,\delta A + 24.71\,\delta D - 28.72\,\delta\omega - 82.17 = 0$$
$$+ 24.71\,\delta A + 184.66\,\delta D - 3.16\,\delta\omega - 439.51 = 0$$
$$- 28.72\,\delta A - 3.16\,\delta D + 484.51\,\delta\omega + 21.72 = 0$$

Their solution gives—

$$\delta A = + 1.''181 \pm 0.''202$$
$$\delta D = + 2.''225 \pm 0.''070$$
$$\delta\omega = + 0.''0397 \pm 0.''0418$$

Every photograph gives, likewise, one equation of condition in position-angle, p, of the form

$$0 = a'\,\delta A + b'\,\delta D + c'\,\delta\omega - (0'. - C'.)$$

The normal equations in p are—

$$+ 8682117 \quad \delta A - 1404261 \quad \delta D - 138999.20\,\delta\omega - 142109.4 = 0$$
$$- 1404261 \quad \delta A + 1521370 \quad \delta D - 25093.11\,\delta\omega + 10442.1 = 0$$
$$- 138999.20\,\delta A + 25093.11\,\delta D + 7326.76\,\delta\omega + 2651.6 = 0$$

Their solution gives—

$$\delta A = + 1.''109 \pm 0.''109$$
$$\delta D = + 0.''637 \pm 0.''224$$
$$\delta \omega = + 0.''0252 \pm 0.''0595$$

Combining these values of δA, δD, and $\delta \omega$ in accordance with their probable errors, we have, finally,

$$\delta A = + 0.''075 \pm 0.''006$$
$$\delta D = + 2.''083 \pm 0.''067$$
$$\delta \omega = + 0.''035 \pm 0.''034$$

The assumed value of ω being 8.''848, we have, therefore, for the mean equatorial horizontal parallax of the sun,

$$8.''883 \pm 0.''034,$$

corresponding to a distance between the centres of the sun and earth, equal to 92,028,000 miles.

(This paper appears in part in *The American Journal of Science* for June, 1881.)

Mr. HARKNESS remarked that the Americans who were engaged in the last transit observations may fairly congratulate themselves upon the results obtained from the photographs, as he had no doubt that they were more satisfactory and consistent than the photographic results obtained by any other nation. There may be said to be two distinct methods of obtaining photographs involving instruments differing widely from the other. The English method employed a telescope of four or five inches aperture producing an image of the sun about three-fourths of an inch in diameter. It is necessary to enlarge this image to a diameter of about four inches, and therefore they used in connection with it a Dallmeyer rapid rectilinear lens, enlarging it by that amount. It is obvious that this enlargement by the use of such a lens must be accompanied by an amount of distortion of the image, which, unless it can be accurately determined and eliminated, must introduce a serious error in the measurements of the negatives, and in the results derived from them. This distortion varies in the direction of radii from the optical center of the image, and is equal in circles about that center. Thus far the amount of this distortion has not been determined. The other method, employed by the Americans, involved the use of a lens with forty feet focal distance giving directly the required size of image, and involving no appreciable distortion inherently due to the construction of the apparatus, and thus avoided the causes of error just described. The focal length required to be determined with great accuracy, and this was readily effected.

Another difficulty arose from the fact that the diameter of the photographic picture on the negative was liable to variation, with a varying length of exposure; and the diameter of the image of Venus is liable to an inverse variation of the same kind. If the distance between the exterior boundaries of the sun and planet were measured, this error would be liable to vitiate the result and, hence, it was necessary to find the centers of the two images, and measure the distances between these central points. Mr. Harkness described the method by which this was satisfactorily accomplished.

There were about twenty plates which gave anomalous results. It was obvious after trial, that the difficulty was with the plates themselves and not due to the observers, since from any one plate a number of observers obtained corresponding results.

Mr. Harkness then spoke of the various methods employed to ascertain the sun's parallax : 1st, by measuring the velocity of light, and the time required for light to traverse known chords of the earth's orbit; 2d, by measuring the aberration of light; 3d, by measuring the parallax of the planet Mars ; and 4th, by the analysis of the motions of the moon ; all of which gave results in very close agreement.

The second communication was by Mr. G. K. Gilbert on

THE ORIGIN OF THE TOPOGRAPHICAL FEATURES OF LAKE SHORES.

This communication was reserved by the author.

After remarks by Mr. Antisell, the Society adjourned.

202d Meeting.   June 11, 1881.
              The President in the Chair.

Fifty-seven members and visitors present.

The minutes of the last meeting were read and adopted.

The Chair announced to the Society that the General Committee had resolved that at the conclusion of the present meeting the Society would stand adjourned until the second Saturday in October.

The first communication of the evening was by Mr. J. J. Woodward, the President of the Society, entitled

A BIOGRAPHICAL SKETCH OF THE LATE DR. OTIS.

GEORGE ALEXANDER OTIS, Surgeon and Brevet Lieutenant-Colonel, United States Army, Curator of the Army Medical Museum, and Editor of the Surgical volumes of the Medical and Surgical History of the War of the Rebellion, died at Washington, D. C., February 23, 1881, at the comparatively early age of fifty years.

Surgeon Otis was descended from a cultivated New England family. His great grandfather, Ephraim Otis, was a physician who practiced at Scituate, Massachusetts. His grandfather, George Alexander Otis, was a well-known citizen of Boston, Massachusetts, whose early years were occupied by commercial pursuits. Mr. Otis was a man of education and literary tastes, who, so soon as his circumstances permitted, retired from business, and devoted himself entirely to books. He is remembered especially on account of his translation of Botta's History of the War of the Independence of the United States of America, published in 1820, an undertaking in which he was encouraged by James Madison and John Quincy Adams, and which he accomplished so well that the book ran through twelve editions. He died at an advanced age in June, 1863.

The father of Surgeon Otis, also George Alexander Otis, was born in 1804. He attended the preparatory course at the Boston Latin School, studied and graduated at Harvard College, after which he devoted himself, with much promise, to the profession of law. Mr. Otis was married February 9, 1830, to Anna Maria Hickman, of Newton, Massachusetts, daughter of Harris Hickman, a lawyer, born at Front Royal, Virginia, who had enjoyed an excellent professional reputation in early life in the Shenandoah Valley, and subsequently at Detroit, in the then Territory of Michigan. Of this marriage the subject of our biographical sketch was the only issue, Mr. Otis dying of consumption, June 18, 1831.

George Alexander Otis was born in Boston, Massachusetts, November 12, 1830. Left an infant to the tender care of his widowed mother, his early years were nurtured by a devoted love, which accompanied him through youth and manhood, smoothed the pillow of his last illness, and followed him to the grave.

When old enough to go to school, George was sent at first to the Boston Latin School, and afterwards to the Fairfax Institute, at Alexandria, Virginia, where he was prepared for college. In 1846 he entered Princeton College as a student of the sophomore class, and graduated with the degree of A. B., in 1849. Princeton conferred upon him the degree of Master of Arts in 1852.

At Princeton, Otis appeared as a slender, rather delicate youth, of highly nervous organization, whose literary tastes were not satisfied with the comparatively narrow curriculum of his Alma Mater. Always standing well in his college classes, that he did not take a still higher place was not due to lack of ability or of studious habits, but rather to his love of general literature, and the large proportion of his time expended in its cultivation. He had already acquired a fondness for French literature, which he never afterwards lost, and a taste for verse so far cultivated that when he came to graduate the Faculty assigned to him the task of preparing the commencement-day poem. Retiring and reserved in his manners, often silent and abstracted, the few who were admitted to his intimacy found his nature gentle and sympathetic, and several of the friendships he then formed lasted throughout his life.

By this time Otis had selected medicine as his profession. After leaving Princeton he went to Richmond, Virginia, where his mother was then residing, and began his studies in the office of Dr. F. H. Deane, of that city. In the fall of 1849 he proceeded to Philadelphia, and matriculated in the Medical Department of the University of Pennsylvania. That institution conferred upon him the degree of Doctor of Medicine in April, 1851. In those days the medical teachings of the University of Pennsylvania were shaped in no small degree by the influence of the Schools of Paris. Indeed, this was then true of almost all American medical teaching, and ambitious American medical students still looked with enthusiasm towards the lecture-rooms and hospitals of the French capital as affording the richest opportunities for the completion of their medical education. Accordingly Otis spent in Paris the first winter after he graduated in Philadelphia. He sailed from New York on the 16th of August, and reached Paris in the latter part of September, 1851.

During his stay in Paris, Otis made diligent use of the opportunities afforded for professional improvement. A manuscript note-book left among his papers shows that he devoted much time to the clinical teachings of the great French masters of that day. He listened to the instructions of Louis, Piorry, Cruveilhier, and Andral. It was at the time his expectation to give especial attention to the subject of ophthalmic surgery, and accordingly he attended with great diligence the clinics and didactic lectures of Desmarres, but he found the attractions of general operative surgery too strong to permit exclusive attention to this chosen branch, and he continually watched the operations, and listened to the lessons of such surgeons as Nélaton, Civiale, Malgaigne, Jobert (de Lamballe), Roux, and Velpeau. Moreover, the popular excitement which preceded the coup d'état of December 2, 1851, and the probability of bloodshed, directed his attention to the subject of military surgery. Already, November 4th, his note-book records a morning spent at the library of l'Ecole de Médecine in the study of Baron Larrey's "Mémoire," with which he was so well pleased that he at once purchased a copy for closer study. After the coup d'état a considerable number of those wounded at the barricades were carried to the hospitals for treatment, and Otis was thus enabled to take his first practical lessons in military surgery from Velpeau, Roux, and Jobert (de Lamballe).

Meanwhile, however, his diligence in medical studies did not prevent him from spending many pleasant hours in the art galleries and museums, where he found much to gratify his æsthetic nature. Moreover, he took a deep interest in the stirring panorama of French politics, as is shown by a series of letters he took time to write to the *Boston Evening Transcript*.

In the spring of 1852 Otis returned to the United States, reaching New York in the latter part of March. Immediately after his return he established himself at Richmond, Virginia, where he opened an office for general medical and surgical practice, and where his tastes and ambition soon led him to embark in his earliest enterprise in the domain of medical literature. In April, 1853, he issued the first number of *The Virginia Medical and Surgical Journal*. Dr. Howell L. Thomas, of Richmond, was associated with him as co-editor, but the financial risk was assumed entirely by Otis. The journal appeared monthly, each number containing over eighty pages octavo, the whole forming two annual volumes, commencing respectively with the numbers of April and October. It was handsomely printed, and contained from time to time a fair share of original articles, chiefly by physicians residing in Richmond and other parts of Virginia; but its most striking characteristic was the number of translations and abstracts from current French medical literature which appeared in its pages. Dr. Thomas, like his colleague, was a good French scholar, and had studied in Paris; both took part in the labor of translation and condensation, and as most of the articles were unsigned, it is not always possible to ascribe particular ones to the proper editor.

Notwithstanding its merits several causes contributed to interfere with the financial success of the journal. On the one hand, it was unsupported by the influence and business connections of an established publishing house, or of the faculty of any medical college. On the other hand, the success it might perhaps otherwise have achieved as a local organ of the medical profession in Virginia was impaired by the existence of an already-established rival, *The Stethoscope*, a monthly medical journal edited by Dr. P. Claiborne Gooch, at that time Secretary of the Medical Society of Virginia.

The field of local patronage was not large enough to support two such journals, and both suffered from the competition. Before the close of 1853, Otis found it necessary to secure an associate who could share in the pecuniary support of his enterprise. Thomas retired from the editorship, and was succeeded after the issue of the December number, by Dr. James B. McCaw, of Richmond, who became also part owner of the journal. *The Stethescope* appears to have suffered still more, for about the same time its editor entered into negotiations with the Virginia Medical Society, as a result of which he sold the journal, and the number of *The Stethescope* for January, 1854, appeared as "the property and organ of the Medical Society of Virginia, edited by a committee of the society."

This arrangement was, undoubtedly, for a time very prejudicial to the prosperity of the *Virginia Medical and Surgical Journal*, but its editors bravely maintained the struggle, and in the heated discussion concerning the purchase of *The Stethoscope*, that took place during the meeting of the Medical Society of Virginia in April, 1854, Otis, with characteristic gallantry, refused to surrender his independence to secure the passage of resolutions complimentary of the managment of his journal.

Otis had, by this time, become dissatisfied with his prospects of professional success in Richmond, and circumstances led him to select Springfield, Massachusetts, as his place of residence. He removed to that town during the summer of 1854. This necessitated changes in the management of the *Virginia Medical and Surgical Journal*. In May, 1854, Dr. J. F. Peebles, of Petersburg, Virginia, became associated with McCaw as one of its editors, while Otis retired from active participation in its direction, retaining, however, literary connection with it as corresponding editor.

Meanwhile, a single year proved sufficient to disgust the Virginia Medical Society with the task of editing a journal. Its management was found fruitful of unfortunate dissensions, and in May, 1855, the society wisely concluded to sell out. Under new auspices *The Stethoscope* continued to appear monthly until the close of the year, when an arrangement was effected by which it was united with *The Virginia Medical and Surgical Journal*, under the title of *Virginia Medical Journal*, with McCaw as editor, and Otis as corresponding editor.

Although his residence in Richmond had failed to secure for Otis a lucrative practice, this could not well have been expected at his early age. It had, however, given him some opportunities for acquiring experience at the bedside as well as in literature, and if he did not secure the profitable favor of the laity, he at least won for himself the respect and confidence of his professional brethren. He was an active member of the Virginia Medical Society, and represented that body in the American Medical Association at the Richmond meeting of May, 1852. He was also a member of the Richmond Medico-Chirurgical Society, which he represented in the American Medical Association at the New York meeting of May, 1853.

Established at Springfield, Massachusetts, Otis occupied himself more exclusively than heretofore with the duties of private practice, and with better pecuniary success than he had enjoyed at Richmond. He continued for a time to contribute translations, abstracts, and various items to the *Virginia Medical Journal;* but as the demands of his business became more urgent these became fewer, although he continued to be nominally corresponding editor of that journal until the close of 1859. As time wore on, he began to obtain considerable local reputation as a skillful surgeon, and would probably have acquired both wealth and distinction in civil surgical practice but for the outbreak of the War of the Rebellion. This changed the whole tenor of his life. So soon as it became clear to his mind that the struggle was likely to be a prolonged one, he resolved to devote himself to the service of his country. He received from Governor Andrew the appointment of Surgeon to the 27th Regiment of Massachusetts Volunteers, of which Horace C. Lee was Colonel, and was mustered into the service of the United States, September 14, 1861.

The 27th Regiment was raised in the western part of the State of Massachusetts, and was mustered into the service of the United States at Springfield. It left the State November 2, 1861, and proceeded by rail to the vicinity of Annapolis, Maryland, where it went into camp. Here it remained until January 6, 1862, when it was embarked on transports, and accompanied the North Carolina Expedition under General Burnside. It took part in the affair on Roanoke Island, February 8th; landed near Newburn, North Carolina, March 13th, and met with considerable losses during the battle of Newburn on the following day. The regiment remained in North Carolina until October 16, 1863, when it embarked for Fortress Monroe, Virginia, and after a short encampment at Newport News, proceeded to Norfolk, Virginia, where it remained through the following winter.

During almost the whole of this time Surgeon Otis accompanied his regiment and shared its fortunes; sometimes, indeed, performing other duties in addition to his regimental ones, as during the summer and fall of 1862, when he acted as Medical Purveyor to the Department of North Carolina. The exceptional periods were a few days in September, 1862, when he went as medical officer in charge of the steamer "Star of the South" with sick from Newburn to New York, and a few months in the early part of 1863, when he served on detached duty in the Department of the South. While in the Department of the South he attracted the attention of Surgeon Charles H. Crane, U. S. Army, then Medical Director of the Department (afterwards Assistant Surgeon-General of the Army), on whose recommendation he was placed, March 28th, by command of General Hunter, in charge of the hospital steamer " Cosmopolitan," then at Hilton Head, South Carolina, and directed the operations of that vessel in the transportation of the sick and wounded within the limits of the department until May 10, when he was ordered to carry a number of sick and wounded to New York harbor, and after landing them, to turn over the vessel to Surgeon Wm. Ingalls, of the 5th Massachusetts regiment. This order was promptly executed, the vessel was turned over as directed, May 13th, and Otis received a leave of absence for twenty days, at the expiration of which he returned to his regiment.

January 22, 1864, he was again detached and ordered to Yorktown, Virginia, to assume the duties of surgeon-in-chief of General Wistar's command. This responsible position he filled in a satisfactory manner from the first of February, when he reported for duty at Yorktown, until April 11, when he was relieved and assigned as surgeon-in-chief to General Heckman's division of the 18th Army Corps, then encamped near Portsmouth, Virginia. May 10th he received a sick leave for fifteen days, which, as his health was not restored at its expiration, was extended for thirty days more. June 26, 1864, he tendered his resignation as surgeon of the 27th Massachusetts regiment, and received an appointment as Assistant Surgeon of United States Volunteers, to date from June 30, 1864.

At this time business connected with his resignation and re-appointment brought Otis to Washington, where he renewed his acquaintance with Surgeon Crane, then on duty in the Surgeon General's Office. Surgeon Crane, while Medical Director of the Department of the South, had been most favorably impressed with the culture and ability of the Massachusetts surgeon, and now so effectually commended him to the Acting Surgeon General as to induce that officer to ask his detail for duty in his office. An order to that effect was issued by the Secretary of War July 22, 1864; and Otis was immediately assigned as an assistant to Surgeon John H. Brinton, U. S. Volunteers, at that time Curator of the Army Medical Museum, and engaged in the duty of collecting materials for the Surgical History of the War of the Rebellion. August 30, 1864, Otis was promoted to the rank of Surgeon of Volunteers, and October 3, 1864, was ordered to relieve Surgeon Brinton of his various duties.

From the first, Otis devoted himself with signal zeal and ability to the large and important duties of his new position. Immediately after he took charge of the Surgical Division he inaugurated a system of record books, which proved ultimately of great service in securing the accurate and complete record of individual cases for use in the Surgical History. The rapidly increasing surgical collection of the Army Medical Museum also received great attention from him, and he expended much time in its supervision and study.

Immediately after the close of the war, the Surgeon General of the Army became desirous of securing, by appropriate legislation, the funds necessary to complete and publish the Medical and Surgical History of the War. Accordingly he called upon Otis, and his colleague, Woodward, who had charge of the collection of materials for the Medical History and of the medical branches of the

Museum, to make reports on the extent and nature of the materials collected for the purpose in question. These reports were published by the Surgeon General November 1, 1865, as "Circular No. 6," for the year 1865. This circular was widely distributed, attracted great attention at the time, and satisfactorily attained the object which led to its publication. It formed a quarto volume of 166 pages, with a number of illustrations intended to indicate the character of those regarded as desirable for the Medical and Surgical History. The first half of the volume was occupied by the Surgical Report prepared by Otis. It was a thoughtfully prepared document, which excited the universal admiration of military surgeons in Europe as well as in America.

It became necessary after the close of the war to retain many of the staff surgeons of volunteers in the service for duty in the general hospitals or other purposes after the great armies had been disbanded, and Otis was, of course, retained with that rank as long as possible; but it was foreseen that the great work he had commenced would occupy a number of years, and he was induced to make arrangements for entering the army as an assistant surgeon. Accordingly he passed the examination prescribed by law, and February 28, 1866, received an appointment as Assistant Surgeon, U. S. Army, but he was not finally mustered out of service as surgeon of volunteers until June 4, 1866, and hence did not accept his commision as Assistant Surgeon U. S. A., until the 6th of that month.

Meanwhile Otis was devoting himself to the study and arrangement of the materials collected for the Surgical History with indefatigable energy, and while engaged upon that work received authority to publish two preliminary studies on special subjects connected therewith, which greatly increased the reputation he had won by his report in Circular No. 6. The first was *A Report on Amputation at the Hip-joint in Military Surgery*, published as Circular No. 7, Surgeon General's Office, July 1, 1867. In this he not merely presented and analyzed the histories of the several amputations at this joint reported to the Surgeon General's Office during the civil war, but discussed with the critical abilities of a master the whole literature of the subject so far as it was at the time accessible to him. An examination of this monograph shows that he had already pretty well begun to emancipate himself from the leading-strings of the French school, and had fully acquired the desire, so

manifest in his subsequent work, to compare and weigh all accessible human knowledge on each branch of his subject before arriving
at his own conclusions.

These characteristics were, if possible, still more fully displayed
in the second of the studies referred to: *A Report on Excisions of
the Head of the Femur for Gunshot Injury*, published as Circular
No. 2, Surgeon General's Office, January 2, 1869; a monograph in
which the subject was treated in a manner similar to that of Circular No. 7, but with a still greater wealth of literary resources.
The appearance of each of these monographs was welcomed with
acclamations of praise, in which the authoritative expressions of
approval by the recognized masters of European surgery were
united with the encomiums of the American military surgeons.

Great interest in the forthcoming Surgical History of the War
was excited by these publications, and very high expectations were
formed, which, however, were fully realized by the character of the
First Surgical Volume. This volume was issued in 1870. It treated
of the special wounds and injuries of the head, face, neck, spine,
and chest, was richly illustrated, and discussed the vast amount of
material collected during the civil war, in connection with the several subjects treated, with characteristic learning and ability. The
Second Surgical Volume was issued in 1876. It treated of the
wounds and injuries of the abdomen, pelvis, back, and upper
extremities. Fully equal in interest and execution to the first volume, it was much more voluminous. The two volumes represent a
prodigious amount of patient labor on the part of the editor. The
extremely favorable manner in which they were received in surgical
circles at home and abroad is well known.

During the interval between the appearance of these two volumes, and subsequently, Otis found time to prepare and publish
several valuable reports on subjects connected with military surgery,
of which the most important were: *A Report of Surgical Cases
treated in the Army of the United States from 1865 to 1871*, issued as
Circular No. 3 from the Surgeon General's Office, August 17, 1871,
*A Report on a Plan for Transporting Wounded Soldiers by Railway
in time of War*, Surgeon General's Office, 1875; and *A Report on
the Transport of Sick and Wounded by Pack Animals*, issued as Circular No. 9 from the Surgeon General's Office in 1877. A full list
of his official and other publications would occupy too much space
to be presented in this place.

In the midst of this successful but laborious career, during the month of May, 1877, his health, never very robust, gave way, and, although he survived for several years, he was a constant invalid, to whom death came in the end as a welcome release from suffering. He was engaged at the time of his death on the third surgical volume, which he has left in an unfinished condition; a colossal fragment that must require great labor to complete in a manner worthy of the first two volumes.

Otis received the appointments of captain, major, and lieutenant-colonel by brevet, to date from September 29, 1866, "for faithful and meritorious services during the war." He was promoted to be surgeon in the army, with the rank of major, March 17, 1880. He was elected a foreign member of the Medical Society of Norway, October 26, 1870; a foreign corresponding member of the Surgical Society of Paris, August 11, 1875; and an honorary life member of the Massachusetts Medical Society in February, 1877. He was also at the time of his death a member of the Philosophical Society of Washington, and of the Academy of Natural Sciences of Philadelphia.

In expressing his high appreciation of the character and value of the surgical works of his late colleague, the writer of these pages does but echo the universal language of competent critics throughout the civilized world. On all sides the opinion has been expressed that they have not only made the name of Otis illustrious, but have reflected the greatest credit upon the intelligent liberality of the Government of the United States, and upon the Medical Corps of the Army.

During his connection with the Museum, Otis always took deep interest in the anatomical collection, now embracing about two thousand human crania. As early as January, 1873, the Surgeon General at his instance made a fruitless endeavor to procure an appropriation for the publication of an illustrated catalogue of this valuable collection. To facilitate this object Otis prepared a check-list of the specimens, which was printed in 1876, but the pecuniary means for preparing and publishing the larger work have not yet been provided.

Until his last illness Otis retained much of the fondness for polite literature which characterized him in early life. He had, moreover, considerable taste for music and the fine arts. These qualities made his companionship charming to those who enjoyed his intimacy.

Hesitating, often embarassed, in his manner in ordinary conversation, especially with strangers, he became eloquent when warmed by the discussion of any topic in which he took interest, and he took interest in a great variety of subjects besides those directly connected with the work of his life.

Many warm personal friends share the grief of his family at his untimely death, which, as has been well said by the Surgeon-General, "will be deeply deplored not only by the Medical Corps of the Army, but by the whole medical profession at home and abroad."

LIST OF THE PUBLICATIONS OF G. A. OTIS, M. D., ETC.

Case of Pericarditis in a child of four years and seven months of age. [Reported to the Medico-Chirurgical Society of Richmond, March 1, 1853.] The Virginia Medical and Surgical Journal, Vol. I, 1853, p. 33.

On Hemorrhage from the Umbilicus in new-born Infants. Same Journal, Vol. II, 1853, p. 49.

A Report of a Case in which an Enlargement of the Isthmus of the Thyroid Body was successfully extirpated. Same Vol., p. 115.

On the Per-chloride of Iron in the Treatment of Aneurisms. [Remarks appended to a translation of an article by *Malgaigne* : "De l'emploi du perchlorure de fer dans le Traitement des Anéurismes." L'Abeille Médicale, Octobre, 1853, p. 292 *et seq.*] Same Vol., pp. 295 and 497.

On the Local Treatment of Erysipelas. [Abstract of remarks made in the Medico-Chirurgical Society of Richmond, January 17, 1854.] Same Journal, Vol. III, 1854, p. 13.

Translation, with Notes, of Velpeau's Review of the Surgical Clinique of La Charité, during the Scholastic Year of 1853-4. [Translated from Le Moniteur des Hopitaux, 1854, p. 801 *et seq.*] Same Journal, Vol. IV, 1855, pp. 31, 111, and 321, and Vol. V, 1855, pp. 213, 298, and 378.

Remarks and Excerpts relating to Variola and Vaccinia. Virginia Medical Journal, Vol. VII, 1856, p. 109.

On Strangulated Hernia in Children. Same Journal, Vol. X, 1858, p. 201.

Letter to the Surgeon General of Massachusetts on the Sanitary Condition of the 27th Mass. Vols., from Camp Reed, near Springfield, Mass., October 5, 1861. The Boston Medical and Surgical Journal, Vol. 65, 1862, p. 204.

Letter to the same, on the same, from Camp Springfied, near Annapolis, Md. Same Vol., p. 435.

Letter to the same, from Newbern, N. C., March 28, 1862, [giving an account of the participation of the regiment in the battle of Newbern, and of his management of the wounded.] Same Journal, Vol. 66, 1862, p. 237.

The Surgical portion of (pp. 1-88) *Circular No. 6, War Department, Surgeon General's Office. November 1, 1865.* Reports on the extent and nature of the materials available for the preparation of a Medical and Surgical History of the Rebellion. Printed for the Surgeon General's Office by J. B. Lippincott & Co., Philadelphia, 1865, 4to., pp. 88.

Circular No. 7, War Department, Surgeon General's Office, Washington, July 1, 1867. A Report on Amputations at the Hip-joint in Military Surgery. 4to., pp. 87.

Observations on some Recent Contributions to the Statistics of Excisions and Amputations at the Hip for Injury. The American Journal of the Medical Sciences, Vol. LVI, July, 1868, p. 128.

Rejoinder to a Reply to a Review of Dr. Eve's Contribution on the History of Hip-joint Operation. The Buffalo Medical and Surgical Journal, Vol. VIII, August, 1868, p. 21.

Circular No. 2, War Department, Surgeon General's Office, Washington, January 2, 1869. A Report on Excision of the Head of the Femur for Gunshot Injury. 4to., pp, 141.

Medical and Surgical History of the War of the Rebellion, 1861–1865, Part 1, Vol. II, being the First Surgical Volume. Washington, Government Printing Office, 1870, 4to., pp. 650. Second issue, 1875.

Circular No. 3, War Department, Surgeon General's Office, Washington, August 17, 1871. A Report of Surgical Cases treated in the Army of the United States from 1865 to 1871. 4to., pp. 196.

Memorandum of a Case of Re-amputation at the Hip, with Remarks on the Operation. The American Journal of the Medical Sciences, Vol. LXI, January, 1871, p. 141.

A Report on the Plan for Transporting Wounded Soldiers by Railway in time of War. Washington, Surgeon General's Office, 1875, 8vo., pp. 56.

Description of Selected Specimens from the Surgical Section of the Army Medical Museum at Washington. [International Exhibition of 1876.] Gibson Bros., Washington, 1876, 8vo., pp. 22.

Description of the U. S. Army Medicine Transport Cart, Model of 1876, prepared in conjunction with Brevet Lieutenant Colonel D. L. Huntington, Assistant Surgeon U. S. A. [International Exhibition of 1876.] Gibson Bros., Washington, 1876, 8vo., pp. 16.

Check-List of Preparations and Objects in the Section of Human Anatomy of the U. S. Army Medical Museum. [International Exhibition of 1876.] Gibson Bros., Washington, 1876, pp. 135. Second edition, Gibson Bros., Washington, 1880, 8vo., pp. 194.

Medical and Surgical History of the War of the Rebellion, 1861–1865, Part II,
    being the Second Surgical Volume. Washington, Government Printing
    Office, 1876, 4to., pp. 1024. Second issue, 1877.

Circular No. 9, War Department, Surgeon General's Office, March 1, 1877.
    A Report to the Surgeon General on the Transport of Sick and Wounded
    by Pack Animals. 4to., pp. 32.

Report of a Board of Officers to decide on a Pattern of Ambulance Wagon for
    Army Use. [Prepared by him as recorder of the board.] Washington,
    Government Printing Office, 1878, 8vo., pp. 79.

Contributions from the Army Medical Museum. Boston Medical and Surgical
    Journal, Vol. XCVI, March, 1877, p. 361.

Article *Surgery* in Johnson's New Universal Cyclopædia. New York, A. J.
    Johnson & Son, 1878, Vol. IV, pp. 1678–1686.

Notes on Contributions to the Army Medical Museum by Civil Practitioners.
    Boston Medical and Surgical Journal, Vol. XCVIII, February, 1878, p.
    163.

Recent Progress in Military Surgery. Same Vol., April, p. 531.

Photographs of Surgical Cases and Specimens, taken at the Army Medical Mu-
    seum, with Histories of three hundred and seventy-five cases. Washington,
    Surgeon General's Office, 1866. 1881, 8 vols., 4to.

The next communication was by Mr. ALEXANDER GRAHAM
BELL

UPON A MODIFICATION OF WHEATSTONE'S MICROPHONE AND ITS
APPLICABILITY TO RADIOPHONIC RESEARCHES.

In August, 1880, I directed attention to the fact that thin disks
or diaphragms of various materials become sonorous when exposed
to the action of an intermittent beam of sunlight, and I stated my
belief that the sounds were due to molecular disturbances produced
in the substance composing the diaphragm.* Shortly afterwards
Lord Raleigh undertook a mathematical investigation of the subject,
and came to the conclusion that the audible effects were caused by
the bending of the plates under unequal heating.† This explanation has recently been called in question by Mr. Preece,‡ who has

* Amr. Ass. for Advancement of Science, Aug. 27, 1881.
† Nature, Vol. XXIII, p. 274.
‡ Roy. Soc., Mar. 10, 1881.

expressed the opinion that although vibrations may be produced in the disks by the action of the intermittent beam, such vibrations are not the cause of the sonorous effects observed. According to him the ærial disturbances that produce the sound arise spontaneously in the air itself by sudden expansion due to heat communicated from the diaphragm; every increase of heat giving rise to a fresh pulse of air. Mr. Preece was led to discard the theoretical explanation of Lord Raleigh on account of the failure of experiments undertaken to test the theory.

He was thus forced, by the supposed insufficiency of the explanation, to seek in some other direction the cause of the phenomenon observed, and, as a consequence, he adopted the ingenious hypothesis alluded to above. But the experiments which had proved unsuccessful in the hands of Mr. Preece were perfectly successful when repeated in America under better conditions of experiment, and the supposed necessity for another hypothesis at once vanished. I have shown in a recent paper read before the National Academy of Science,* that audible sounds result from the expansion and contraction of the material exposed to the beam, and that a real to and fro vibration of the diaphragm occurs capable of producing sonorous effects. It has occurred to me that Mr. Preece's failure to detect with a delicate microphone the sonorous vibrations that were so easily observed in our experiments, might be explained upon the supposition that he had employed the ordinary form of Hughes' microphone shown in Fig. 1, and that the vibrating area was confined to the central portion of the disk. Under such circumstances it might easily happen that both the portions (A B) of the microphone might touch portions of the diaphragm which were practically at rest. It would, of course, be interesting to ascertain whether any such localization of the vibration as that supposed really occured, and I have great pleasure in showing to you to-night the apparatus by means of which this point has been investigated. [See Fig. 2.]

The instrument is a modification of the form of microphone devised in 1827 by the late Sir Charles Wheatstone, and it consists essentially of a stiff wire, (A,) one end of which is rigidly attached to the centre of a metallic diaphragm (B.) In Wheatstone's original arrangement, the diaphragm was placed directly against the ear

---

* April 21, 1881.

Fig 1.

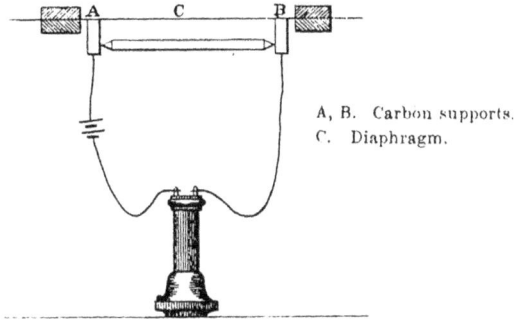

A, B. Carbon supports.
C. Diaphragm.

Fig 2.

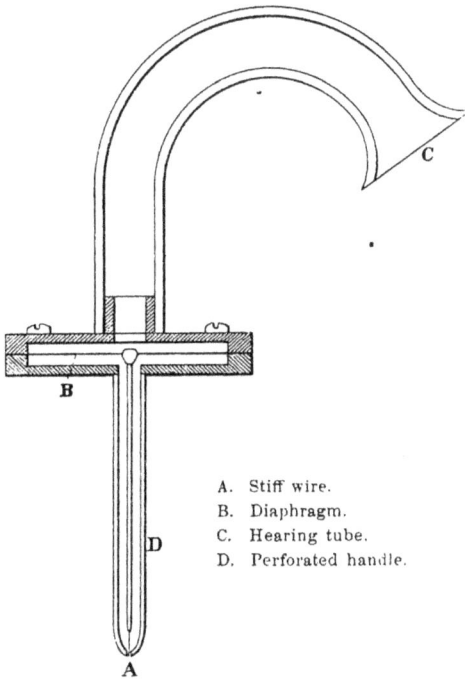

A. Stiff wire.
B. Diaphragm.
C. Hearing tube.
D. Perforated handle.

and the free extremity of the wire was rested against some sounding body, like a watch. In the present arrangement the diaphragm is clamped at the circumference like a telephone-diaphragm, and the sounds are conveyed to the ear through a rubber hearing-tube (C.) The wire passes through the perforated handle (D,) and is exposed only at the extremity. When the point (A) was rested against the centre of a diaphragm, upon which was focussed an intermittent beam of sunlight, a clear musical tone was perceived by applying the ear to the hearing-tube (C.) The surface of the diaphragm was then explored with the point of the microphone, and sounds were obtained in all parts of the illuminated area, and in the corresponding area on the other side of the diaphragm. Outside of this area on both sides of the diaphragm the sounds became weaker and weaker until at a certain distance from the centre they could no longer be perceived.

At the points where one would naturally place the supports of a Hughes' microphone [see Fig. 1,] no sound was observed. We were also unable to detect any audible effects when the point of the microphone was rested against the support to which the diaphragm was attached. The negative results obtained in Europe by Mr. Preece may, therefore, be reconciled with the positive results obtained in America by Mr. Tainter and myself. A still more curious demonstration of localization of vibration occurred in the case of a large metallic mass. An intermittent beam of sunlight was focussed upon a brass weight (1 kilogram,) and the surface of the weight was then explored with the microphone shown in Fig. 2. A feeble but distinct sound was heard upon touching the surface within the illuminated area, and for a short distance outside, but not in other parts.

In this experiment, as in the case of the thin diaphragm, absolute contact between the point of the microphone, and the surface explored was necessary in order to obtain audible effects. Now, I do not mean to deny that sound waves may be originated in the manner suggested by Mr. Preece, but I think that our experiments have demonstrated that the kind of action described by Lord Raleigh actually occurs and that it is sufficient to account for the audible effects observed.

The next communication was by Mr. J. M. TONER on

EARTH VIBRATIONS AT NIAGARA FALLS.

In June, 1874, the speaker, in company with Dr. J. D. Jackson, of Kentucky, visited the Clifton House on the Canada side of Niagara. On the night of his arrival he was kept awake by the illness of his companion, and his attention was drawn to the frequent rattling of the doors and windows of his room. He was first led to suppose, while speculating upon the cause, that the vibration might be due to pulsations in the air produced by the falling water ; but upon further reflection concluded that it could not be satisfactorily explained in that way, as it continued independently of the direction of the wind. On the following day he made it the subject of conversation with others, but no one seemed to agree with him. He had occasion, however, to note when his chair was tilted back against the stone wall of the house that a tremulous motion, or grating was perceptible. At the time this tremor was a novelty to him, but subsequently he had met with allusions to it by several writers. He was led to the following explanation, viz: that the fall of such a large body of water through so great a vertical distance, must necessarily impart vibrations to the massive rocks which form the trough of the river above and below the falls, and that these vibrations are transmitted through the earth itself. To test this theory, he made on the next day the following experiments: A large carving dish holding water was placed on the rock between the falls and the hotel. Upon the water was poured some sweet oil, and it was seen that wave-rings appeared on the surface of the water. These rings were made more distinct by placing a mirror so as to view them by reflection. No rhythm was detected in these vibrations. The dish was placed in many localities, more than thirty in number, and at varying distances from the falls. Waves were observed in it from the Burning Spring above the falls, and as far as half a mile below the small suspension bridge. They were also noted on the steps of the little Episcopal Church, a mile west of the Hotel on the Canada side. Similar results were obtained on the American side.

At the conclusion of Mr. Toner's remarks the Society adjourned to October 8th.

INDEX.

187